instant
magick

About the Author

Christopher Penczak is an award-winning author, teacher, healing practitioner, and eclectic witch. His practice draws upon the foundation of modern witchcraft blended with the wisdom of mystical traditions from across the globe. He has studied extensively with witches, mystics, and healers in various traditions to synthesize his own practice of witchcraft and healing. He is an ordained minister, herbalist, flower essence consultant, and certified Reiki Master (Teacher) in the Usui-Tibetan and Shamballa traditions. He is the author of several books, including *The Inner Temple of Witchcraft, The Temple of Shamanic Witchcraft, Gay Witchcraft,* and *Magick of Reiki.*

ancient wisdom

modern spellcraft

instant
magick

CHRISTOPHER
PENCZAK

Llewellyn Publications
Woodbury, Minnesota

First Edition
First Printing, 2006

Book design by Donna Burch
Cover art © BrandX Pitures & Digital Vision
Cover design by Kevin R. Brown
Edited by Andrea Neff
Interior illustrations by Gavin Dayton Duffy

Llewellyn is a registered trademark of Llewellyn Worldwide, Ltd.

Library of Congress Cataloging-in-Publication Data

Penczak, Christopher.
    Instant magick : ancient wisdom, modern spellcraft / Christopher Penczak.—1st ed.
      p.   cm.
    Includes bibliographical references and index.
    ISBN-13: 978-0-7387-0859-1
    ISBN-10: 0-7387-0859-3
     1. Magic. 2. Charms. I. Title.

    BF1611.P465 2006
    133.4'3—dc22
                                      2005055174

Llewellyn Publications
A Division of Llewellyn Worldwide, Ltd.
2143 Wooddale Drive, Dept. 0-7387-0859-3
Woodbury, Minnesota 55125-2989, U.S.A.
www.llewellyn.com

Printed in the United States of America

Other Releases by Christopher Penczak

City Magick: Urban Spells, Rituals and Shamanism
(Samuel Weiser, 2001)

Spirit Allies: Meet Your Team from the Other Side
(Samuel Weiser, 2002)

The Inner Temple of Witchcraft:
Magick, Meditation and Psychic Development
(Llewellyn Publications, 2002)

The Inner Temple of Witchcraft Meditation CD Companion
(Llewellyn Publications, 2002)

Gay Witchcraft: Empowering the Tribe
(Samuel Weiser, 2003)

The Outer Temple of Witchcraft: Circles, Spells and Rituals
(Llewellyn Publications, 2004)

The Outer Temple of Witchcraft Meditation CD Companion
(Llewellyn Publications, 2004)

The Witch's Shield
(Llewellyn Publications, 2004)

Magick of Reiki
(Llewellyn Publications, 2004)

Sons of the Goddess
(Llewellyn Publications, 2005)

The Temple of Shamanic Witchcraft
(Llewellyn Publications, 2005)

The Temple of Shamanic Witchcraft Meditation CD Companion
(Llewellyn Publications, 2005)

Forthcoming Releases by Christopher Penczak

The Mystic Foundation
(Llewellyn Publications, 2006)

Ascension Magick
(Llewellyn Publications, 2007)

Special thanks to my husband, Steve, my parents, Ronnie and Rosalie, Leandra Walker, all of my students, and most especially Laurie Cabot.

Contents

List of Exercises   *viii*

List of Figures   *ix*

Introduction   *1*

Chapter One: What Is Instant Magick?   5

Chapter Two: The Anatomy of a Spell   13

Chapter Three: The Worlds of Magick   29

Chapter Four: Instant Magick Spells   61

Chapter Five: Spellcrafting   101

Chapter Six: Advanced Instant Magick   113

Chapter Seven: Instant Healing   131

Chapter Eight: The Magickal Life   155

Appendix: Correspondence Charts   *161*

Bibliography   *199*

Index   *201*

Exercises

Exercise 1: Altering Consciousness   16

Exercise 2: Sensing and Manipulating Energy   23

Exercise 3: Elemental Connection and Balance   34

Exercise 4: Spirit Guides Meditation   39

Exercise 5: Weaving Meditation   44

Exercise 6: Rising Through the Chakras   51

Exercise 7: Rising Through the Planetary Spheres   56

Exercise 8: Programming Your Instant Trigger   63

Exercise 9: Higher-Self Connection   111

Exercise 10: Inner Magick Circle Ritual   116

Exercise 11: The Inner Temple   122

Exercise 12: Heartbeat Control   133

Exercise 13: Breath of Fire   135

Exercise 14: Cooling Breath   136

Exercise 15: Positive Breathing   137

Exercise 16: Negative Breathing   138

Exercise 17: Elemental Breathing   139

Exercise 18: Pranic Breathing   142

Exercise 19: Pore Breathing   144

Exercise 20: Inner Temple Healing   153

Figures

Figure 1: Elements on the Pentacle   33

Figure 2: World Tree   37

Figure 3: OM Symbol   41

Figure 4: Astrological Wheel   42

Figure 5: Web of Life   43

Figure 6: Chakras   47

Figure 7: Planes of Existence   49

Figure 8: Ten-Pointed Star with Planetary Symbols   56

Figure 9: Tree of Life   59

Figure 10: Banishing Pentagram   71

Figure 11: Caduceus   109

Figure 12: Astrological Glyphs for Mercury and Venus   109

Figure 13: The Hand and the Elements   141

Figure 14: Color Wheel   149

Introduction

Contrary to the title, *Instant Magick* is not a book of quick, easy spells that require no energy, effort, or imagination. It is not a simple recipe book guaranteed to make your life perfect with a few herbs, crystals, or candles. Magick doesn't work that way, though we often wish it would.

Magick is a path of transformation, healing, and awareness. *Instant Magick* is a book that will help you weave the natural energies of life through your will, words, and visions into a transformation. The initial results can seem instantaneous. You will an event to occur, and it occurs. The process of magick is to explore your will, and through it, to weed out the unwanted, unhealthy, and unnecessary desires to find your true will, the desire of your soul.

I'm a practical person, and think the exploration of your true will should have practical applications. The traditions of magick I have studied are about learning to go with the flow of nature, and gently shape it to aid your journey. With a knowledge of magick, you will swim with the stream of life rather than against it.

The spells of *Instant Magick* are not your typical pagan or ceremonial spells. They don't involve complicated rituals. They don't involve altars and magickal tools. You don't need candles, special ingredients, or exotic symbols. I love those spells, and have used them before and will use them again, but there are many times in life when you need to tap in to your energetic awareness and create change. You can't always get to your altar, and many times you need magick in your car, at work, or on the run. The spells here are accessible at any time, through meditation, visualization, words, and intent. Many practitioners gain a greater awareness of energy as they practice traditional magick, and learn to adapt their will-working techniques to many different traditions. They do magickal workings similar to those in *Instant Magick*, yet their magickal training only included education in traditional spellcraft and formulas.

You don't have to be involved in traditional magick to use this book, but it doesn't hurt. It is for beginners, but can also provide new methods for the experienced practitioner. An understanding of magick aids the study of any technique. You don't have to come from a specific belief system, such as modern paganism, witchcraft, or ceremonial magick, though we'll be using elements from those traditions. My background is in these forms of Western magick, so of course they will be a part of my magick and writing. We won't, however, be using traditional spellcraft techniques, so you don't need to buy any tools, herbs, or crystals. All you need is yourself.

I'm not a fan of traditional spell books, and I'm not a fan of teaching people to just do spells. I like magick books, and I like teaching people how to do magick, to understand the discipline, theories, and practice of it. I don't like teaching pieces. It's the difference between teaching someone how to cook, and how to cook just one thing, with no idea how the process works. If you stick to one recipe or one spell, you are fine, but if you venture from that one familiar territory, you are out of luck because you don't have the fundamentals. I like to teach people the foundation, so they can make their own magick.

Instant Magick is a different kind of spell book. Though it contains recipes, they're not the typical ones you've seen before. The ingredients are nontangible, but just as effective. The first chapters will teach you the fundamental concepts of traditional magick. The nontangible ingredients are the energies that correspond to the traditional colors, candles, herbs, and stones. Through working with these energies on a primal, intuitive level, rather than through more traditional ingredients such as herbs or stones, you will understand the fundamentals of all spellcraft and take your magick in any direction you desire. Use the spells in this book as inspiration to create your own spells. Work with your own understanding of magick to fill your personal needs and find the path of your true will.

chapter one

What Is Instant Magick?

Instant magick is a technique to create change in your life in the simplest way possible. Modern mystics define magick as creating change in your reality with the power of your will. You intend something to happen, and it occurs. Traditionally, such magick is executed through ritual.

Rituals can be simple or complicated, depending on the tradition. Some are acts of folk magick and require only household tools. The actions involved seem fairly ordinary, but when done with will and intent, they become a magick ritual. Things like cooking, sewing, gardening, dancing, singing, or even playing with dolls or sticks can be incorporated into folk magick.

A lot of our superstitions devolved out of folk magick. Common practices like throwing a pinch of salt over your shoulder when the salt shaker spills may seem random, but there is a magickal theory at the root of these traditions. Early on my path, I was told by a practitioner that salt naturally absorbs harmful energy. Salt is used in all manner of protection spells. When the salt shaker spills, it would be surmised that harmful energy was around you. It could have been a malicious thought or word from someone else, what those in folk traditions think of as the "evil eye" when done intentionally to cause harm. The salt was "reacting" to the harmful energy. To get rid of the harm, you throw the substance that attracted the harm—the salt—behind you, to put it to your past, not before you, to your future. Once you understand the reasoning behind this custom, it no longer is a superstition, and becomes a ritual of magick.

Complicated rituals are found in other traditions, from formalized systems of Wicca to ceremonial magick. Even most mainstream religious services have their basis in older, more mystical rituals. Such rites involve special words and movements, with and without specific ritual tools, done in a specific manner. The magickal orders of witches and magicians have their tried and true methods of doing spells, specific acts of magick. Though some magickal practitioners divide witchcraft and Hermetic magick into low and high forms of magick, both can be quite complicated in their own right—they are just different.

These more complex paths are based on systems of correspondence. In magick, all things relate to each other. Certain objects share qualities with certain ideas and intentions. The light of the sun can be seen in the shining metal gold. The two are related, just as the light of the moon is seen in the metal silver. The sun and moon are symbolic of male and female, projective and receptive, rational and intuitive. The correspondence systems build upon these qualities, forming intricate cosmologies and theories. These systems relate intentions with astrology, symbols, herbs, stones, colors, and metals. By matching your intention with the proper rituals, tools, and timing, you create a powerful spell.

Instant magick takes the best qualities of both these systems and merges them into a harmonious whole. The technique uses the simplicity of folk magick and the art and logic of the correspondence-style systems, but instead of focusing on the outer tools, the focus is brought back to the inner tools. The practitioner's ability to sense and manipulate energy and his or her connection to the divine are the greatest tools of all.

In complicated forms of magick, and even in aspects of simple folk magick, the preparation involved in gathering the necessary tools prevents the practitioner from using magick in day-to-day life, for routine needs. Instant magick makes magick instantly accessible. The results are not always instant, but with some of these spells you will feel an immediate difference as soon as you do them.

Immediate change occurs most often when you change the inside reality first. Most practitioners of spellcraft focus on using ritual to create a change in the environment and the people around them. Most of the spells in this book focus on using energy to produce a change in you, the spell caster, rather than in the outside world. When you change your inner reality, you change your viewpoint and the way you relate to the outer world. If you transform your relationship with the situation in the inner world, you will transform the situation in the outside world. If you practice magick long enough, you will realize what mystics have known for centuries—that there is very little difference between the "outside" world and the "inside" world. Both the inner and outer worlds are simply points of view, and to the mystic, each is equally valid.

Let's say you are in a situation where a coworker is doing something that really bothers you. It might be a perfectly acceptable action, like constantly tapping his foot, but it annoys you. As time goes on, it bothers you more and more. You ask him to stop, but it's an unconscious habit, so he always falls back into it even though he doesn't mean to do it. It distracts you from your own work. What do you do?

Most beginning practitioners would do a spell to make their coworker stop the annoying habit permanently. Though in the larger view foot tapping is pretty trivial, a new magician would feel powerful and proud if he successfully stopped it.

Some practitioners would argue that to perform such a spell would be unethical, because you would be violating this person's free will to tap his foot if he so chooses. He's not hurting anyone. They would have a point, too.

Your last option should really be your first option. You could change yourself, change your reaction pattern, so that the foot tapping no longer bothers you. You have the greatest sovereignty over yourself—use it. We are here to master ourselves as well as to influence the outer world. If you are bothered and annoyed by your coworker, chances are it has little to do with the foot tapping. You are probably upset about something else and are simply venting your frustration in this small way, making a mountain out of a molehill. If you really had the magickal power most magicians claim to have, little things would not bother you.

You could choose to see this person as a spiritual teacher urging you to look inside and use magick upon yourself. Our antagonists, big and small, can be our greatest teachers.

Many people forget that magick is all about change, and the greatest change is in the inner, not outer, landscape. Outer magickal changes—such as immediately getting a new job, money, a lover, or physical healing—seem more impressive at first, but the inner changes last longer. They are the most impressive. Anyone can learn to do some basic spells and have good results, but the practitioners who develop a solid spiritual and magickal practice and become more centered, calm, healthy, and truly confident over time are the magicians who impress me.

Instant Magick contains spells of change for both the inner and outer worlds, but you should never forget that you are the connecting point between the two. Your relationship to these worlds is where the strongest magick manifests. Some outward spells take longer to manifest in the physical world. Your desired result might not be instantaneous, but doing magick gives you the ability to take responsibility for actively changing your reality. If you understand the connection between your inner and outer realities, magick can transform a situation where you feel helpless into one where you feel empowered. Magick gives us the tools to act when problems arise. Other times, the outer manifestation of a spell is almost instantaneous. Many witches and mages have had the experience of doing a spell to receive a communication from a distant, out-of-touch friend, and then getting a call or letter from the person later that day.

At first glance, the techniques of instant magick may seem to consist of nothing more than basic self-help skills, including affirmations and creative visualization. I see that such modern takes on magick, found in corporate boardrooms and recovery groups, are actually harnessing more ancient principles of magick. My interest in instant magick grew out of an understanding of these modern views of magick. The first "spells" I learned in witchcraft were much like the ones found in this book. They involved will, intent, a light meditative state, and quick visualizations. They have served me well to this day.

Then I met other witches who told me I wasn't doing "real" magick and that I didn't know "real" spellcraft. To them, spells were the recipes they copied out of their teachers' magickal book of rituals, called a Book of Shadows. They felt that such spells were more valid because they were traditional and passed on through secrecy, yet these particular witches didn't have a great understanding of how and why they worked. They simply followed the recipes. Since my technique was more fluid and imaginative but lacked the esoteric words and ingredients, it didn't seem like real magick to them.

I knew my magick worked, but I still felt inadequate compared to my counterparts who had received more traditional training. I felt like I was missing something, so I continued my studies in more traditional directions. I learned systems of correspondence. I learned formal ritual. I learned astrology and herbalism. All of these techniques are wonderful and valid, and I do use them, but I still found myself going back to my daily, quick spells. I found myself expanding upon them and adding to them, using the knowledge of more complicated forms of magick yet not adding physical tools. I went beyond simple visualizations and affirmations, though they are still the foundation of my magickal practice. As I became more sensitive to energy, I moved into using my will with energy. My visualizations became more abstract, more symbolic, though they were just as powerful. I weaved my knowledge of, and most importantly, my growing relationship with, the elements, planets, colors, and deities into my acts of instant magick.

Through these experiments, my magickal awareness grew. My understanding grew. My spirituality grew. Through a merging of the aspects of magick that were most important to me, I found a path that I could use whenever and wherever I desired.

At the time I thought I was quite special for expanding upon these basic techniques, but then I found out that I was not the only one doing so. Though some techniques and ways of doing things may be particular to me and my own unique thought process, I discovered that the basic idea of instant magick—of energetic magick with some form of correspondences but without physical tools—was being used by many practitioners. I know a few practitioners who focus on chant. Others petition deities or spirits to obtain results. Many more still just focus on the energy of their desire. But all these techniques work, and all are forms of instant magick.

The idea of doing magick without tools isn't as new and modern as one might think. Doreen Valiente, best known as Gerald Gardner's high priestess and arguably the mother of modern Wicca, wrote about it in her book *Natural Magic*. In the chapter titled "Magic of the Mind," she tells the story of Karagoz:

> In the late eighteenth century there lived a remarkable man called Mehmet Karagoz. He was known as the Wizard of Albania. People from all over Europe and Asia sought his advice and told stories of his supernormal powers. He was born in the wild and remote mountains of Tartary, and his father was a shaman, a magician-priest of the private religion of those parts.
>
> When he was a young man, Mehmet seemed to be so lacking in natural ability that his father felt unable to have him initiated, thinking that the youth was incapable at that time of following his father's vocation. Instead, the old shaman gave Mehmet a piece of practical instruction: "Believe in the possibility of what you intend to do, hold it strongly in your mind, and it will happen." He told his son to practice constantly and one day he would find that the power had indeed developed and was his.
>
> This instruction of his father's was the foundation of Mehmet Karagoz's magical career. He traveled widely in search of knowledge and eventually settled in Albania, where he founded his own occult school and became one of the most famous and most mysterious of adepts. He used no rituals, but worked entirely through the powers of the mind.
>
> —*Natural Magic*, p. 17

The story of Karagoz illustrates how the most important factors in magick are belief and mental focus, rather than physical tools, and that they have always been a part of magick. This book will continue the tradition, as I will expand upon the mind-magick techniques of the past to give you more inner tools to focus your will to shape both your inner and outer realities.

Through learning these techniques, you will discover what aspects of instant magick work best for you. You don't have to use them all. Don't be overwhelmed by the choices. The variety of options gives you the freedom to choose what works for you. Follow your intuition. See what sparks your magickal curiosity. What raises the hairs on the back of your neck or sends a shiver down your spine? That's where you will find your magick. Then you will have the knowledge and skills to create your own instant spells, to be used whenever you need to create a change in your life.

chapter two

The Anatomy of a Spell

When you have no knowledge of magick, looking at a book of spells is much like looking at a book of chemical formulas with no knowledge of chemistry. From the old translated Greek papyri and alchemical texts to the most modern kitchen witchcraft book, the words, colors, and ingredients seem to be randomly mixed together. There is some inherent order, some rhyme and reason, yet if you don't know the codes and correspondences, it makes no sense. The thought of really doing your own spells seems impossible.

With any complex problem, when you take it apart and look at one section at a time, it becomes easier to understand. When you take a spell or ritual apart and understand how the parts work together as a whole, the craft of magick becomes much clearer.

Although there are many variables to magick, the anatomy of a spell consists of three basic components, regardless of the tradition or ritual. The three components are:

1. Altering consciousness

2. Focusing will

3. Directing energy

As long as you include all three components in your spellcraft, you can use any style of techniques that suits you. The spell will still work. If you are missing any aspect, then your spell is not likely to manifest. It's like missing a vital organ. The whole cannot be sustained.

Working with these three components is the creative aspect of ritual design. Each tradition and, in fact, each ritual has its own way of altering consciousness, focusing intention, and manipulating energy. Ritual is the technology, the vehicle, that you use to do spell work. Just as most cars have the same basic machinery to get you from point A to point B, rituals also have the same basic machinery.

The difference is in the style. Not all cars look and feel the same way. We each have our preferences. You may have a favorite color, manufacturer, or model of car. Some people like convertibles, and some like controlled air conditioning. Sometimes we make choices based on economic restraints. We do not always get what we would want in our wildest fantasies, but rather what is practical.

It is the same with spell work. Our fantasy of working magick might be dancing naked around a bonfire, deep in the forest, on the night of the full moon. It's a wonderful way to work magick if you can arrange it, but most of us can't, at least not regularly. Practically speaking, we need a style of magick that we can do in our own home, and in the quiet moments of the day. Fire dances and kitchen witchcraft both share the same three components. Both have a history of successful spellcraft. The difference is in the style and practicality.

Altering Consciousness

The first component of a spell, altering consciousness, is often overlooked in modern spell casting. The purpose of most rituals is to alter consciousness. When we change our mindset, our relationship to the inner and outer worlds, we find that place within our consciousness, that inner still point where the mind is clear and focused, in alignment with our will, and our magick is most effective. That inner still point is the foundation of magick. When we are immersed in and distracted by our cluttered thoughts and daily concerns, we cannot find that still point to do our magick. The techniques of altering consciousness bring us out of day-to-day focus, allowing us to step between worlds, step out of space and time, and work with magickal energies. We can still be aware of the regular world, and still function in it, but our focus, our anchor in reality, has shifted. Most people set their anchor, their connection to reality, only in the physical world. Magicians can move their connection to the realities beyond normal space and time. When we shift our "reality anchor," moving from the physical to the unseen worlds beyond the limits of space and time, the endless possibilities of magick open up to us. We sense a reality that was invisible to us before, and new worlds open up to us.

Altered consciousness may seem to be an elusive state achieved only by mystics and gurus, but technically "altering consciousness" refers to changing your consciousness from where it currently is at to a new and different level. In spell casting and magickal meditation, altering consciousness refers to purposely shifting your brain-wave state from a level that scientists call beta, indicative of someone wide awake and alert to physical reality, to lower brain-wave states known as alpha, theta, and delta. Most people daydream, lose focus, and ultimately lose consciousness at these lower brain-wave states, but the magician seeks to keep focus. Alpha level is the easiest altered state to be in and still remain focused. It is a relaxed state that includes daydreaming as well as the trancelike states induced by repetitive dancing and music. We all float in and out of the alpha state of consciousness all the time. The difference between having a daydream and doing magick is that with magick you have conscious control of the switch between the various states of consciousness. This is the art of altering consciousness.

Repetition and structure in thought, word, and movement are the elements that create altered consciousness in ritual. Many Eastern mystical traditions use the repetition of a mantra as a meditative focus. One sacred sound, one word or phrase, is repeated silently over and over again. When it is spoken or sung, the mantra becomes a chant. Western magickal traditions also use words of power, and many eclectic practitioners just repeat their magickal or mundane name over and over again. Some people count their breaths. You can stare at a visual focus, called a yantra or mandala, to induce an altered state. All the senses, not just sound and sight, can help create a new awareness. Candles, incense, oil, food, and drink play a part in many different types of ceremonies. All of the various rituals, both in meditation and magick, are designed to induce an altered state.

Any ritual designed to induce an altered state must have boundaries. It must help you enter and cross the first boundary, and actually succeed in getting you into an altered state. This is not as hard as it sounds. Sitting in a dark room with your eyes closed, breathing deeply, will get you into an alpha state usually within less than five minutes.

The ritual technique must have a way of ushering your return back to ordinary consciousness. The method must ground you back into physical reality, into the here and now, and not leave your awareness in an altered state.

With these thoughts in mind, create your own ritual to enter an altered state of consciousness. Make it something you can do almost anywhere to focus your awareness. Look at the following exercise as an example to inspire you.

Exercise 1

Altering Consciousness

Sit down comfortably and close your eyes. You can light a candle or incense or play soft music to help you relax, but you don't have to do so. Ultimately, you will want to be able to alter your consciousness anywhere, under any circumstances, but if you are just starting out, do whatever you think will help you create a relaxed feeling.

Bring your awareness to the top of your head, and scan your body, bringing your awareness down slowly from the crown to the feet. As you pass each body part, give it permission to relax. Be aware of resistance and stress, and when you find such places, imagine waves of relaxation flowing from your crown, through these zones, sweeping them clear of all unwanted energies. Allow yourself to relax fully, to the best of your ability.

Breathe deeply. Take slow, full breaths that fill your lungs completely, then gently release the air. Try to make each inhalation and exhalation a little longer than the last. Feel the breath like a gentle wind, blowing back and forth. Imagine any distracting thoughts in your mind as clouds, and gently blow them away with your breath. Don't obsess about them or try to control them. Just let the winds of your mind sweep them away, until your mind is like a clear sky.

Focus on your heart. Feel the energy in your chest. Feel the beat of your heart and the flow of your blood. Feel the love you hold in your heart. Feel the love you have for family and friends, the love you have for the divine spirit, and the love you have for yourself. Within your heart and soul, feel your own spark of divinity, like a flame that will guide you in your magickal journeys. You don't have to see anything in your inner vision. Just know it's there and acknowledge its presence.

Through this centering ritual you have acknowledged the four traditional elements of magick. Relaxing the body helps you attune to the earth element, which rules your physical body. Clearing the mind by focusing on the breath attunes you to the air element, which rules your thoughts. Focusing on your heart, blood, and the love you feel is symbolic of the water element, and feeling the spark of your soul is for the fire element. This centering ritual alone is enough to alter your consciousness, but it can also prepare you to go even deeper.

Next, with each breath, count down from twelve to one. I imagine that my mind's eye is like a movie screen or chalkboard, and then I draw the number twelve, erase it, then draw eleven, erase it, and so on, until I reach one. This activates my more active, analytical mind, and focuses it on the task at hand. Then I count down from thirteen to one, not visualizing anything but simply listening to my inner voice, activating my receptive, intuitive mind in the process.

After both countdowns, you will be in an altered state of consciousness. Take a few moments to simply enjoy this state of mind. Feel yourself aware, yet relaxed. Focused, yet open. This is the meditative state. These two countdowns are only one way to get to this state, but this technique is very effective for modern magick workers.

Affirm that you are in your meditative state, a state where all magick is possible if it is for the highest good, harming none. Your magick is in accord with your true will.

When you are ready to come out of this state, reverse the process that brought your brain waves down to this level. Count up from one to thirteen, then count up from one to twelve. You don't have to visualize the numbers this time. Normalize your breath. Feel your body. Wiggle your fingers and toes. Move your limbs. Stretch. Activate your physical energy.

If you feel spacy, what most people call "ungrounded," at the end of the exercise, you have several options. You can simply wait and center yourself. You can press your hands down onto the floor, "earthing" any excess energy and helping you get in contact with the physical world. You can imagine that your feet are like the roots of a tree, anchoring you, or that you have a string of light descending from the base of your spine into the earth, tying you down like a balloon. You can eat or drink something to speed up your metabolism and bring your energy back into your physical body, or you can hold something that has grounding magickal properties, such as most dark stones, like hematite, smoky quartz, or black tourmaline. Once you feel grounded, you can return to your normal routine.

Practice this skill of altering consciousness daily until you are well versed in it. The technique will come in handy for future acts of instant magick and meditation.

Clear Intention and Divine Will

What do you want? Do you really want it? Have you thought about what it entails and how your life will change once you have it? If you can't answer these questions easily, then you do not have the second requirement of magick—clear intention. You must know what you want before you set the wheels of creation in motion. You can do magick without clear intention and get results, but it's not very smart. The result you get may not be what you really wanted.

Intention is the focus of your will, your primal energy used to create. Will relates to the element of fire and the ritual tool of the wand. The magick wand directs our will. Fire is the spark of creation, the spark of life within us. It is the divine, godlike essence. As the divine force is a creator, we too are partners in the creation process. This divine force is the fire that fuels your creation. If you don't know how, where, or why you are directing your will, you will never get the results in magick that you desire. Most people are not clear in their intentions, so their will is often thwarted, and they see no other options in life and feel out of control, victimized, or at the whims of fate. An understanding of will and intention is what separates magick workers from ordinary people. We all have the same potential. We all create our own lives, our own realities. Those who do magick are simply more educated and active in working with their inborn gifts. They are conscious of their creations.

In studying magick, you will learn about two very different and distinct forms of will. First there is your personal will, what most people think of when they hear the word will. It is what you want on a personal, ego level. It is influenced by your hopes, dreams, fears, and past successes and failures. Personal will is not good or bad. It's simply a part of existence. We all have a personal will.

The second is your divine will, known as true will, magickal will, or higher will. This is what your soul, your higher self, wants for you. It is the true "you" beyond this time, place, and body. It is the bornless, eternal self. Your true will helps you fulfill your role in the divine plan. It is your life's purpose. We each have many purposes, on many different levels and in many different situations. Our true will regarding our family and relationships might be very different from our true will regarding our career. We can be clearly expressing our true will in one aspect of life and not in another, yet our true will in one aspect of life will support us in finding our true will in all other areas of life. Each aspect of our true will supports the others.

Our true will changes over time. What is appropriate at one point may not be at a later date. My experience as a musician and singer reflected my true will for a short period in my life, and at the time I was supported in that endeavor by my magick. I learned a great deal about public speaking and overcoming stage fright, which has served me well in my magickal writing and lecturing. It was not appropriate for me to remain a professional musician for my entire life. My true will called me to other work.

Many practitioners believe that real magick only involves rituals and spells that support, encourage, and express your true will. If your magickal intention is not in harmony with your true will, then you are not doing magick, or at the very least you are not doing good magick. Magick that derails you from your true purpose but is done with the intention of the highest good, harming none, often just fails. We can do magick with the disclaimer "I ask that this be correct and for the highest good," or something similar, to short-circuit spells that conflict with our divine true will.

Though some people choose to do harmful and malicious magick, out of harmony with their true will, their spells are shortsighted and will eventually turn back upon them. Magick stemming from true will is on a higher vibration than harmful magick, or magick stemming from pure ego. Magick that is not of the true will is not necessarily harmful. Magick is a technology. If you have the proper technique, intention, and energy, you can create almost anything. The question is, should you? Sometimes, exploring desires that are not for the highest good eventually points us in the direction of true will. We might be attracted to the light and heat of a fire, not knowing that it's a mistake to touch it, and get burned. Once we do that and get burned, we know not to do it ever again. Some of us instinctively know not to do harmful magick, as many of us know not to play with fire. Some of us have that self-preservation instinct, while others have to learn the hard way. Ultimately, magick stemming from the intention to express our true will is much more effective.

When we work magick, we find our true will by examining what is supported and what is not. We work through our desires, discovering what is healthy and what is not. We work through our fears, blocks, and ego. Those spells that do not manifest usually are not for our highest good, and we can more fully examine why we wanted to do them in the first place. By noting the spells that work best, we find experiences that support our higher will. If a spell doesn't work, we also have to consider our technique and spellcraft before assuming it wasn't for our highest good. There is a science behind magick, and if we choose to work with tools that conflict with our intention, then our spell will fail.

You might wonder, why do magick at all? If we have a divine will, doesn't that mean things are meant to happen? If we are supported by divine will, why take action? What about fate, or destiny? On the magickal path, we believe that divine will has a pattern, but we have free choice as to how we will manifest that pattern. Divine will supports us, but through magick, we invite it into our lives. We become active, not passive, partners in its manifestation. We create our reality with it. To fully express our divine will, we need to be conscious participants in our reality, with clear intentions. We are free to explore and express our true will. Because of the general lack of introspective and intuitive skills taught in our society, it is difficult to even have an understanding of our true will, and we take a lot of time exploring it.

The highest aspect of magick is merging your personal will (what you want) with your divine will (your life's purpose). Through magick, Western mages and witches have their own path to awakening and enlightenment. Though magick is practical and designed to bring balance to your life, it is also very spiritual, though the spiritual side of magick is often overlooked in the instructions on how to make potions and charms found in most spell books. Magick is a spiritual partnership, a cooperative effort.

Before you do any magick, even a seemingly simple spell, ask yourself a few initial questions. First of all, is this something you really want, or do you want something different? Many people do magick for the means to an end rather than for the ultimate goal, when doing magick for the goal is far more effective. For example, if you are sick and lack health insurance, don't do a spell for the money to buy your medicine. (Do you really want the money, or the medicine?) Do a spell for the medicine itself. Someone might give it to you free of charge. A government agency might have a program that you qualify to join. There are many possibilities. In fact, I would imagine your ultimate goal would be to get better. If that's the case, then do a spell to get healthy. If the medicine is a part of getting healthy, it will be included in the spell, perhaps with other benefits. Getting healthy might mean getting involved with an herbalist or a nutritionist who agrees to take you on as a client at a low cost. If you did a spell strictly for pharmaceuticals, the energy of the spell would not be free to act and attract the herbalist to your life. Ask yourself what your desired end result is, and once you know, go for that result with your magick.

Have you thought about the consequences of the spell, and how it will change your life? Many people do spells and get exactly what they asked for, only to discover that it wasn't what they really wanted. I know someone who did a love spell to find her perfect husband. She found him, but then was upset that he got so serious so quickly. She thought she would still be able to date other people, but her new boyfriend wanted to get married and settle down right away. She never thought about the implications of finding her husband. She only thought she wanted him. Still, she got exactly what she asked for.

Lastly, ask yourself if the goal of your spell is for your highest good. Does it support your divine will? Is the spell in harmony with your previous spiritual experiences, and will the result aid you on your life's path? Or will the result be contrary to what feels right for you now?

By asking yourself these questions, you will become clear in your intent. You will walk the magickal path of will and learn to understand your needs and desires. You will manifest what is needed, discard what holds you back, and transform your life as you merge with your divine higher will.

Directing Energy

Directing energy is the third and final component of spell casting. Altering your consciousness allows you to perceive and tap in to the subtle energies within and around you. Subtle energies are the unseen forces that sustain our reality. Having a clear intention opens the pathway for what you desire to manifest. Energy direction allows you to gather the necessary energies and launch them into the universe to manifest your will.

You need a method of energy direction. As with altering consciousness, the methods to direct energy are diverse. Different traditions combine a variety of these techniques to make effective magick. Some people use their pure will to gather and direct energy. Once they psychically sense energy, sheer focus and concentration are the only things needed. Movement, postures, and dance are all effective ways to both alter consciousness and work with energy. Visualization is an effective tool for directing energy. Seeing in your mind's eye what you want to manifest is a prime method of programming the energy to do your bidding. Like a mantra, words and sounds focus and send energy. Affirmations, positive statements, and prayers are all methods to manifest. Many prayers end with an affirmation, a statement that what is said is true, such as the Judeo-Christian "Amen." Other traditions have similar words and sounds. In Wicca, we end many spells with "So mote it be," meaning "It is so." Energy is often raised, gathered, and projected through the medium of ritual. Ritual can combine a variety of these magickal techniques fluidly and effectively to create change.

Think about how you perceive and manipulate energy best. What senses and techniques appeal to you? If working with subtle energy is brand-new to you, try this simple energy exercise to get your feet wet. Then experiment on your own.

Exercise 2

Sensing and Manipulating Energy

Sit down in a comfortable position. You don't have to get into a deep meditative state, as in Exercise 1: Altering Consciousness, but you should be relaxed and in a receptive frame of mind.

Raise your arms out and to the sides, palms facing each other. Slowly bring your hands together. With each breath, allow yourself to sense the energy between your hands. The energy will not necessarily grow stronger as you move your hands closer together. You might feel it pass in waves. Some waves will have unique qualities. The energy might be felt like resistance from a magnet, or perhaps in terms of cold and hot temperatures. The experience is very subjective, and everybody feels the energy differently. With practice, you will feel it too.

Once you have a sense of the subtle energy in your own body, play with this exercise using other people, plants, trees, and rocks as your targets. Can you sense their energy? Many people can tune in to one type of energy—say, that of minerals—better than that of people. Learn where your strengths and weaknesses are.

To manipulate this energy, you can use your will, play-acting, and visualization. Repeat the sensing-energy exercise. Bring your hands fairly close together, about six inches apart. Your intention is to create a ball of light between your hands. Imagine that the energy you sense feels like clay, and you are molding the clay into a ball with your will and your hands.

Energy work and breath work are intimately tied together. Breath moves energy. In the ancient worlds, the word for "vital life force" was often linguistically connected to the words for "breath" and "air," based on the common belief that air carries this vital energy. In Hinduism, prana is the life energy related to breath. Pranayama is breath work, specific yogic exercises to build this energy within the body. Breath is related to the mind. Energy moves with the breath and the mind. Calming the breath alters the consciousness, the energy of the mind.

When you want to add to the ball of energy in your hands, imagine breathing through your feet or crown. As you inhale, draw up earth energy from below, or draw down sky energy from above, and feel it circulate through your body, to your arms and out through your hands. Notice the slight differences between the two sources of energy. As you become more skilled at this, you can draw on the earth and sky energies simultaneously.

You can also breathe in slow, long breaths and fast, rapid breaths to feel the energy of the body shift. By exhaling "into" the ball of energy, you can add to its power. Play with the breath, and learn how energy moves with breath and thought.

Imagine the energy as being a specific color. For now, choose your favorite color. All colors have specific properties and intentions. You can experiment to see how the different colors affect you. If in doubt, choose a ball of white light. Make the ball bigger and sturdier as you manipulate it. When done, you can either put the ball of energy into the ground or imagine reabsorbing it into your hands. Later, you will learn how to create and direct this energy for a variety of intentions.

Thoughtforms

Thoughtforms are the building blocks of a spell. They are simply "packets" of energy directed by your will. An altered state of consciousness allows you to sense and manipulate energy. Through using your will, you gather your packet of energy—either literally in your hands, or in your mind's eye. Focusing on your clear intention for the spell, you imprint your intention into the energy. Though such energy packets consist of a variety of energies, they are called thoughtforms because your thoughts, your intentions, rule them. Your intention is like a computer program. The energy moves to fulfill the instructions of your thoughtform to the best of its ability, like a computer running code.

In magick, we create intentional thoughtforms, with specific purposes. When they complete their purposes, they have used up their energy, and any remaining energy breaks down harmlessly to its basic components. Some of these thoughtforms can be crafted into semipermanent constructs that can be periodically "recharged," such as a thoughtform designed to protect a home.

Even if you don't do magick formally, you can unconsciously create thoughtforms. Our hopes, dreams, and wishes can create helpful thoughtforms, much like an unconscious spell. Unfortunately, many people focus on the problems in their lives, and continually create and recharge harmful thoughtforms that broadcast feelings and thoughts about unhappiness, shame, fear, and anger. These thoughtforms eventually become the "block" in a person's energy system that can manifest as mental/emotional imbalance and even physical illness.

A key factor in successful spell casting is learning to let go of your thoughtform, thereby letting go of your intention. If you don't let it go, it can't go out into the universe to create your desired intention. You call it back by thinking about it, worrying about it, or getting upset about it. You drain its energy, taking back its power bit by bit, until it has none to fulfill your intention. Trust that it's working. If you could keep a completely upbeat attitude, and send it more energy, as many people try to do through repeated actions, then you could potentially empower the thoughtform. But for most of us, particularly beginners, our repeated thoughts come with doubts and fears. It's best to learn to let it go completely, and not concern yourself as to how a spell will manifest. Just be confident that it will because you crafted it properly.

Magickal Ritual

Ritual brings together the three components of spell casting. Ritual is the structure where we place all the parts of our craft. Ritual is really a form of technology, allowing us to smoothly integrate the process of altering our consciousness, focusing our will, and raising and directing energy.

In ritual we use symbols, usually a variety of symbols, to speak with the universe. As humans, we cannot process raw magickal energy. We create symbol systems to interpret energy and work with the universal powers. Even when we think we are processing energy directly, we perceive it through symbols of the physical senses. We feel the energy as temperature or magnetism. We physically "see" it as light. We "hear" it as sound. Our senses are symbolic when it comes to subtle energy. Some symbol systems become our spiritual structures and eventually our religions. They are the interface we use to connect with subtle energies.

Wise magick workers realize that all traditions are just that—different interfaces—and that each is equally valid and powerful when used by a knowledgeable practitioner. We each resonate with particular symbols and systems. When we find systems that work for us, or create our own from parts of many traditions, we have a technology, an interface, that allows us to do magick.

A computer-savvy friend of mine compares the different magickal traditions to operating software. There are many different kinds of operating software for a computer. Each has its own style and setup. We are comfortable or familiar with a particular kind of software. We can work with other software, but prefer the one that makes the most sense to us. Often we choose that one intuitively. Its creator's imagination is in harmony with our own. Other times we prefer the first kind of software that we learned, because it is familiar and comfortable. Knowledgeable users can customize their "preferences" and "settings" to create something eclectic and personal. No path, no system, is completely right or wrong. Each is a way of using ritual, of using an operating system, to your best advantage.

Rituals are a set of repeated actions that are symbolic in nature. As a part of our societal upbringing, we already know many symbolic actions and movements, such as holding our arm outstretched, palm out, to symbolize stop, or holding our arms open to signal our desire to hug. These actions are innate to most of us, but many other innate actions carry a magickal connotation. Most of us don't recognize them as magickal because we don't live in an inherently magickal society.

Raising your arms up to the heavens is a natural movement to connect with the energy of the sky, sun, and stars. Bowing down toward the ground connects you to the earth and grounds you. Opening your arms wide puts you in a position to receive energy. Crossing your arms prevents unwanted energy from entering your space. People who feel threatened often fold their arms to cover their heart or solar plexus, places where we can feel vulnerable. All of these movements have symbolic qualities, but they also alter consciousness and energy, whether we realize it or not. Eastern forms of mysticism, including yoga and martial arts, alter consciousness and energy through body movements. Ritual magick uses similar, if not as vigorous, body movements to alter consciousness and move energy.

In the most familiar traditional magick rituals, practitioners use ritual tools along with motions and words. The tools hold both a symbolic power and a literal power. A silver chalice is symbolic of the element of water and of the Goddess energy, but there is a natural vibration to the silver metal and the shape of the chalice. Practitioners also use colored candles, incense, herbs, oils, stones, symbols, and a variety of ritual "weapons" such as the wand, blade, chalice, and shield. Each holds both a symbolic power and an inherent natural vibration that makes it useful in altering consciousness, focusing will, and directing energy. When you hold a symbol of a specific energy, particularly a symbolic tool that has been ritually consecrated, you attract the vibration, the energy, of the concept it symbolizes.

All of these tools are much like the different colors in an artist's paint box. They are the colors a magick worker can choose from to express the art of a spell. Many artists favor particular kinds of pigments, brushes, and canvases. The tools we use in spellcraft reflect our personal tastes and aptitudes as well as our tradition of magick.

The rituals of *Instant Magick* do not employ the conventional pigments of physical tools like candles and incense. Like interpretive dance or musical toning, these rituals use raw emotion, will, and intention mixed with powerful words, visualization, and energy. By learning the techniques of instant magick, you will learn how to create your own magick.

chapter three

The Worlds of Magick

We live in many worlds. Many realities coexist with ours. We simply don't see them. Scientists, too, believe that the entire world is permeated by energy, the electromagnetic energy of the known spectrums. We can see light, but hundreds of different waves and particles move through our world without our notice. We are surrounded by the magnetic energy of the earth's field. We have a variety of radio and television waves conducting communication. Invisible particles from the sun bombard us. We are surrounded by many energetic worlds, but never really notice them. We lacked the technology to explore them fully until fairly recently.

Magick is a technology that allows us to explore the unseen worlds that operate under a different set of principles than the familiar physical world. Many of these worlds are the energetic blueprint for, the foundation of, our physical, known reality. They are all complementary to each other. Just as the worlds of light and sound do not fight for dominance, neither do the subtle magickal energies. Some worlds are more responsive to our thoughts. In these worlds, whatever we strongly think about, whatever thoughts we focus upon, become reality. If you create the proper pattern, and fully energize it, you can manifest your will in the physical universe. Magick is not only the technology to tune in to these foundational realities, but also the tool to create change in these worlds, and eventually our own.

Paradigm

Each magickal tradition has its own view, its own paradigm, that allows the user to connect with these other worlds, these subtle energies, and create change. These paradigms are like the aforementioned computer operating systems that "run" our human hardware. The various techniques of each paradigm are like the programs on our system. Each type of software has its advantages and drawbacks, and we each have one view that we tend to favor over others, just like computer users tend to prefer a particular operating system or program.

Each tradition has a slightly different paradigm, with its own religious beliefs, ethics, and dogma, but they all have many common aspects. Each divides magickal energy into a variety of groups. These subdivisions, like the energies themselves, are usually complementary. Simple subdivisions lead to more and more complex subdivisions, though they all stem from the same source.

It is usually only when comparing some parts of Eastern and Western traditions that you find greater differences, at least at first. On the surface, Eastern traditions seem more passive and Western traditions more active. With further study, you realize that each tradition has a balance of both active and passive teachings. Each tradition explores similar concepts, but approaches those concepts differently, based upon its own cultural views.

The following sections describe five multi-tradition paradigms that can be used by anyone. These paradigms are used extensively by practitioners of a variety of magickal traditions. You don't have to choose one and exclude the others, but the more you practice instant magick, the better able you will be to identify the paradigms that work best for you. Each paradigm gives different energetic correspondences for magick. I believe in having a multi-paradigm approach. Once you truly understand what a paradigm is—a model, a map, a way of looking at things—you will never confuse your map for the terrain again. You will never believe that your paradigm is the one and only truth. It is simply one way of looking at things. Some magicians and witches get so caught up in their own tradition or paradigm that they don't see the possibilities in other viewpoints. A good practitioner can work with many magickal operating systems and programs.

The Elemental Worlds

The universe is composed of five elements—earth, air, fire, water, and spirit. This is a popular paradigm found in many traditions, including alchemy, ceremonial magick, and witchcraft. Western ritual magick is often based on the elemental paradigm, honoring the four directions and the center, symbolic of the four outward elements and spirit in the center.

The elemental paradigm has been greatly misunderstood by most people, particularly with the rise of modern chemistry. The five elements are not obvious in everything, and are not meant to be interpreted literally, like the elements in our modern periodic chart. The truth is that each of the five elements is symbolic. Each represents an energy, an archetype, a force of consciousness more in the domain of the psychologist than the chemist. When scientists look at any object, from a rock to a growing flower, they see no actual fire in it. The blowing wind contains no visible earth. The literal, physical element—the actual stone, atmosphere, water, or flame—best describes the elemental energy named after it, but these physical manifestations of the elements are truly symbolic of the larger metaphysical forces.

Earth

Earth is the element of the physical world. All matter is an expression of the earth element. Anything that can be measured by the physical senses is composed of earth energy. The physical shell of all things is the earth element. Cells, molecules, and atoms are expressions of the earth element. The material world—in fact, the entire material component of the universe—is the expression of the earth element. Earth is the densest of the elements. The physical world is the manifestation of all the elements, though it takes the earth element to manifest something into physical form. Symbolically, the earth in our bodies constitutes the bones and minerals, but technically our entire physical body is an expression of the earth element. The metaphysical concept associated with earth is Law, as the earth element is dominated by the physical laws and structures of the known universe.

Water

Water is the element of shape and form. Our magickal forms are more fluid than our physical forms. Just as water takes the shape of its container, so our water element is shaped by our physical container. It is also shaped by our thoughts and feelings. Water relates to our emotional self, also known as our dream body or astral body. Here we find our self-image. Our astral self is a template for our physical self. When we create changes in the realm of the astral world, the world of form, we create potential patterns to make changes on the physical plane. Though the fluid in our bodies is symbolic of the water element, our emotions and emotional body are truly composed of water elemental energy. The highest expression of water is Love, the highest of emotions and the purest energy to create change through magick.

Air

The element of air is the realm of the mind. Air energy is the idea behind all things. In the magickal laws called the Hermetic Principles, the first principle says that we are all thoughts in the divine mind. All things have a basic idea, a divine thought that eventually creates its form (water) and manifests its form in the world (earth). In living creatures, the air element is expressed symbolically as our breath, but truly it is the mind, the mental body. Elemental air is not only the breath, but also the mental pattern that creates shape in all things, from the geometry of a molecular structure to the blueprint of a building. The sacred principle of air is Life, as air is associated with the breath of life. Air is associated with life force, as in the Hindu term prana. Without this divine thought, nothing could be created or be alive.

Fire

The sacred spark is the element of fire, the most difficult of the first four elements to comprehend. Unlike the previous three elements, the symbol of this energy is not physical. You can hold earth. You can drink water. You can inhale air. But you can't hold fire. You can hold something that is burning, but not the actual flame. Fire is energy, pure potential energy to be put to use. In the physical body, fire manifests as the metabolism, an inner fire that is obviously present yet cannot be touched. But truly, the fire element energy is the spark of divine life within us, the soul. Fire manifests as our passion, drive, and will. Fire is the metaphysical power of Light, the divine illumination that stimulates vision, awareness, and change. Without the fire element, thoughts (air) are not illuminated to take shape (water) and manifest (earth).

Spirit

Spirit is the fifth element, the sum of all four elements yet more than the sum of its parts. Often called quintessence or akasha, spirit is the binding force in which the other four elements manifest. Spirit is the power from which the four elements manifest and to which the four will return. Its job is to keep them all together, yet separate enough to be distinct. I associate spirit with the concept of Liberty, the freedom to pursue your true will.

Figure 1: Elements on the Pentacle

Each of the elements is linked to a ritual tool found in a variety of magickal traditions. You can find these tools in traditions of witchcraft, Celtic legends, and ceremonial magick. Most common images of the four appear in the four suits of the tarot cards. Though this book is not concerned with traditional altar building or tool gathering, we understand that these tools are found within us.

The magickal symbol of the pentacle, a five-pointed star in a circle, is often used for both the element of earth and the element of spirit. The five points are symbolic of all five elements (figure 1). The point on top symbolizes the rulership of spirit over the more terrestrial elements. Other times, the pentacle is described as a coin or shield for the element of earth.

The chalice is the tool of water. The cup is receptive and nourishing. It holds the waters of love and healing. The mythic image of the Holy Grail, the healing cup of divine love, is the ultimate symbol of the water element.

The blade is the ritual tool of air. The blade, either as a ceremonial sword or double-edged blade, is known as an athame in the Wiccan traditions. The blade is symbolic of cutting to the truth, and cutting mental attachments to things that no longer serve. The mythic image of the sword of truth, known as the Sword of Nuada, or the better-known Excalibur, is an embodiment of the air tool.

The magick wand is the symbol of fire. Wands direct your magickal will, directing energy to be used in ceremony or healing. The wand is sometimes substituted with a staff, torch, or spear, depending on the tradition. The Spear of Lugh in Celtic myth is associated with fire, as are the magick wands of traditional magician images such as Merlin.

Exercise 3

Elemental Connection and Balance

Perform Exercise 1: Altering Consciousness to get into a meditative, altered state. On the screen of your mind, imagine a five-pointed star, a pentagram, and know that each point is symbolic of one of the five elements. Through this meditation, you will experience and balance all these energies within you.

As you continue to focus on the inner pentagram, move your awareness to the bottom right-hand point, the point of fire, and feel the pentagram turn red, like a blazing fire. Feel yourself become engulfed in the flames of the pentagram, engulfed in soul fire, and burning away all that hinders your true will. Feel yourself energized and focused. The flames return to the screen of your mind, forming a pentagram again, but you still possess the new vitality and energy they granted.

Move your awareness to the upper left-hand point, the point of air. The pentagram turns yellow and issues forth a strong wind, blowing your hair back but also passing through your body, down to the bone, clearing your mind and body of all unwanted thoughts and unhealthy patterns. You have a fresh, new outlook and a greater sense of creative expression. When the wind dies down, bring your focus back to the pentagram.

Focus your awareness on the upper right-hand point, the point of water. Feel the pentagram turn blue, and crashing through the pentagram comes a wave of saltwater. The water is cold but refreshing. It cleanses your heart and soothes any harmful emotions or past pains from family members, friends, or lovers. You feel filled with pure, unconditional love and a fresh sense of self, like being reborn. The water recedes into the pentagram.

Allow your eyes to flow down to the bottom left-hand corner, the point of earth. The pentagram turns green with your gaze, and as you focus on it, you feel your body begin to crystallize, becoming like a rock. You feel solid and stable, and your perception of your body as rock slowly shifts into a sense of being fertile soil. Your sense of self being like soil recedes down into the ground beneath you, but you still retain the feeling of physical strength.

Finally, bring your eyes to the top point of spirit, and feel yourself immersed in a multicolored white light, like gazing at a shiny opal or through a prism. All colors are present in the energy of spirit, or akasha. Feel yourself protected and balanced by the fifth element.

When done, erase the image of the pentagram from the screen of your mind, and return yourself to normal consciousness.

The Crossroads at the Tree

In the shamanic paradigm, the universe is a great tree known as the world tree (figure 2). The branches reach into the heavens and hold up the stars, and the roots dig deep into the underworld. The trunk lies in the middle world, the realm of space and time. This is the vertical reality of expanded consciousness.

From a psychological perspective, the three worlds represent levels of consciousness. The middle world is the ego, the personal self. The lower world is the unconscious, hidden self. The upper world is the realm of the superconsciousness, beyond the ego and the unconscious. To the mystic, these are not only symbolic of the levels of consciousness within us, but in the divine mind of the universe.

Through ritual, the shaman can consciously go to the tree, which is everywhere, and access the three worlds. The shaman can always stand in the crossroads, the place where the worlds overlap at the base of the tree. The shamanic traditions of native people and of those in the realm of witchcraft overlap. The images of the crossroads, heavens, and underworlds are found in the mythologies of all traditions, even if they are not considered to be classically shamanic.

The key to successfully performing shamanic magick is building relationships with spiritual entities from the three worlds. By working with these spirits, the practitioner can create change. Ideally, one is connecting to all aspects of the self—the middle ego self is aligned with the lower, usually unconscious self and with the higher, divine self. With this alignment, all things are possible. Allies from these realms help the practitioner create such an alignment and manifest change.

Practitioners of spirit magick work with their allies from the various worlds to get information, divine the future, and make change. Shamans call upon their animal and plant allies to bring through spirit medicine to heal and bring balance. The use of spirit in such a magickal manner is not limited to shamanism. We find it in Christian magick as well. Many people will call upon a specific angel or saint who has dominion over a particular area of life. Healing petitions may be said to one being, while a "prayer" for finding lost objects is sent to another. Candles are often lit,

Figure 2: World Tree

or offerings given. We find the same traditions in Voodoo, with the beings known as the loa acting as spiritual intermediaries. Altars are built, and offerings made. Each magickal tradition has its own symbols and correspondences to create an effective petition.

Practitioners of certain traditions of ceremonial magick will not petition the spirits, but summon and bind them. Angels, elementals, spirits, and even demons are summoned to do the magician's bidding. Medieval tomes are filled with spirit correspondences, names, sigils, and rituals to summon and bind spirits.

Some modern traditions of ceremonial magick create magickal constructs—intricate thoughtforms or "artificial" spirits—programmed to perform specific tasks. They function much the same way as the spirits of old, making some magickal practitioners wonder if the spirits of the ancient world are simply intricate, long-lasting thoughtform constructs created by centuries of belief. To others, such thoughts are tantamount to blasphemy, because they believe that each archetype is a pure expression of the divine.

All such spirit-patron practices can be traced back to the polytheistic pagan religions in which a deity has reign over a sphere of life. Each god is a manifested aspect of the creative spirit. The divine creator is too vast to comprehend, so it manifests in more human, more knowable forms. In psychological models, these godforms are often referred to as archetypes, because they appear in so many cross-cultural forms. Each pagan culture envisioned a god of the sky, a god of love, a god of the moon, a god of the sun, a god of truth, and a god of nature. These deities manifest in a variety of forms and genders, but similarities exist between cultures. Even in our modern myths, we still have expressions of the primal mother and father god through the images of Mother Nature and Father Time. Their roots can be found in the stories of Gaia and Chronos.

Working with patron spirits, angels, and deities involves building relationships with the spirit worlds and the divine. In cultures past, practitioners would know, from their cultural mythos, which spirits to petition. In the Greek world, one would call upon Aphrodite for help in love, or perhaps Hermes for help in gambling. Modern practitioners do not have this cultural foundation easily available, since magick is not a part of most people's daily reality, but we now have a rich cross-cultural mythos we can draw upon. Modern practitioners often choose one culture, and remain loyal to it, perhaps based on ancestry or personal interest. Others, myself included, are more cross-cultural, thinking of the entire world as our ancestors, and believing we have a right to all the myths and manifestations of the divine.

The only way to perform spirit magick is to consciously build relationships with your guides and allies in the other worlds. The following exercise will help you make initial contact with these entities, and with continued practice, deepen your relationship with them.

Exercise 4

Spirit Guides Meditation

Perform Exercise 1: Altering Consciousness to get into a meditative, altered state. Imagine a pentagram in each of the four directions around you, charged to protect you from any unwanted energies or influences.

On the screen of your mind, imagine a great tree—the largest tree you have ever seen. It could be an oak, ash, yew, willow, pine, or any tree that speaks to you, but its proportions are gigantic. It reaches up to the heavens and holds the stars in its branches. Its trunk is impossibly wide, as wide as a building. Its roots pass through the planet and deep into the underworlds below.

Imagine that the screen of your mind is like a window or door. It is a portal to the spirit realms. Imagine stepping through the gateway and standing before the tree. Feel the earth beneath your feet. Smell the moist soil. Hear the wind rustle the branches. Reach out and touch the bark. Feel your connection to the world tree.

Walk clockwise around the base of the trunk, and notice that the roots contain all manner of openings, crevices, caves, and tunnels. Look for the opening that calls to you, that intuitively catches your attention. You will know the right one when you see it.

Once you do, enter the dark tunnel. Feel it spiral into the other worlds. You may feel it move downward or upward, depending on what is right for you. Both are acceptable. Feel your pentagrams about you, protecting you. See a light at the end of the tunnel. Enter into the light, and find yourself in a sacred space, out in nature, a place that feels completely comfortable to you. Perhaps it is a place you have visited in your dreams. There, waiting for you, is a guide who is correct and good for you at this time. It might be a humanoid—perhaps a spirit, angel, or ancestor. It might be an animal spirit. Take this time to meet with the spirit and get to know its role in your life. Ask the spirit how it can help you in your magick. This spirit can give you magickal and spiritual advice.

When done, thank the spirit guide, knowing you can always return here and meet with your guide. Return the way you came. Thank the great tree, and step back through the screen of your mind. Erase the image of the world tree, and return yourself to normal consciousness.

The Web of Life

Instead of a world tree, many people look to the image of the spider's web as the symbol of the universe. Each of us is a strand connected to the web of life. Many look to the divine creator as the Weaver Goddess, continually weaving the universe outwardly.

Mythic traditions give us the story of three sisters, three goddesses of fate who weave our lives as they spin the threads of past, present, and future. To the Greeks, they are known collectively as the Moirae, and individually as Clotho, Lachesis, and Atropos. The first goddess spun the thread of your life. The second measures it, allotting the time you will have, and the third will cut the thread of life. Ariadne is also looked to as a weaving goddess, and her name was translated into the weaver-goddess imagery of the Merlin texts of European lore. To the Norse, the three are collectively known as the Norns, or Wyrd sisters, and singly known as Urd, Verdandi, and Skuld—she who was, she who is, and she who will be. The triple-weaver image can be found in the popular Wiccan figure of the triple goddess. Though modern scholars debate the antiquity of the triple-goddess image, we do find triple-goddess themes in ancient lore from many cultures.

The three sisters can be seen as embodying the three universal forces of creation. They are the powers to create, to sustain, and to destroy, as embodied by the maiden, mother, and crone. In Hindu mythology, the same fundamental forces are embodied by male deities. Brahma is the father and creator, Vishnu is the preserver, and Shiva is the dissolver or destroyer. Some dissect the sacred tone OM, more appropriately spelled AUM, and give each of the letters to one of these three primal forces. Even the symbol for OM is reminiscent of the Arabic numeral three (figure 3).

Ritual magicians see the three universal forces of creation embodied in the figures of Isis, Apophis, and Osiris. Isis is the creating force of nature,

Figure 3: OM Symbol

Apophis is the destructive force, and Osiris is the power of regeneration and resurrection. The chant IAO is used to align with these powerful forces. Mystical Christians often interpret the word God (the creator) as an acronym. The G stands for generating, the O for organizing, and the D for dissolving. In astrology, the three principles are described as cardinal, fixed, and mutable (figure 4). When the Sun is in a cardinal astrological sign, a season begins. At these points of the year we have an equinox or solstice. The middle of the season is marked by the Sun being in a fixed sign. The season transitions when the Sun is in a mutable sign. Cardinal, fixed, and mutable are known as the triplicity.

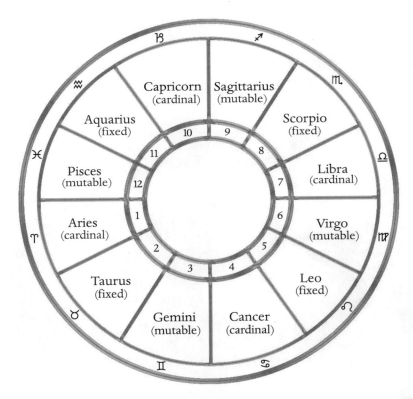

Figure 4: Astrological Wheel

Mystics also tap in to the universal image of webs and weaving—the web of life—to create magick (figure 5). I have worked in my own practice with spider spirits and the weaver goddess, but I thought such practices were particular to me and those with a strong spiritual connection to the spider totem. The web of life is not something found extensively in traditional Wicca, shamanism, or ceremonial magick. Yes, the image is used in a metaphoric sense in many native traditions, but I had not come across much lore encouraging the use of this image in ritual to make magick.

I then corresponded with a few magickal practitioners who imagine the world in terms of a web and perform their instant magick through a ritual of pulling and weaving "strings" of energy in their inner vision. One practitioner felt this technique was only natural, since his patron goddess is a many-armed, spiderlike Hindu deity. Later, I even found the images of weaving and pulling strings to make magick in a magickal role-playing game called "Mage: The Ascension" (White Wolf). In this unusual game, the world is depicted as a tapestry, and mages are the ones who see and can reweave the patterns of reality. The concept of

Figure 5: Web of Life

the web, from ancient mysticism to modern games, is a constant theme. Magick involves patterns and gently changing those patterns in accordance with will. A weaving metaphor is an apt way to manifest these changes.

If you would like to explore the web-weaving paradigm for your own magickal practices, try the next exercise to orient yourself in the web of life.

Exercise 5
Weaving Meditation
Perform Exercise 1: Altering Consciousness to get into a meditative, altered state. Imagine a pentagram in each of the four directions around you, charged to protect you from any unwanted energies or influences. Imagine yourself sitting in the center of a giant web. You are not trapped in the web, but are safely in the center, as if it were your home.

Examine the thickness or thinness of the strands of the web. Note how you feel when you bring your attention to a particular strand. As you look across the astral strands of webbing, notice how each of the major strands is linked to a major person, place, or event in your life. Look down each strand to see what you are connected to—what important factors create your reality? Notice how the strands are not only anchored in the present, but in the past and the future. The web is not just in this moment, but in all the past and all the present. There are too many webs connected with this one to make a full survey of them all, but you are in the center of your web and can create your reality.

Notice how certain strands connected to the past have specific qualities—a certain look or feel. Other strands connected to the present also have certain qualities and characteristics, as do strands reaching into the future. Strands connected to your past, present, and future are not always separate in your personal web. They might entwine or branch out from each other, as your past, present, and future are intimately tied together.

You might find that the web is oriented somewhat like a compass, with major strands in the four or eight directions. More of the strands of the web behind you have a connection to the past, and those strands before you lead to the future. The strands in your web can have other associations, including elemental or astrological correspondences. Use your intuition and extend your awareness down each strand, as if each one was a part of your body. Feel each strand, and try to describe and qualify the feelings, sensations, and thoughts generated through this exploration. You might describe a strand in terms of the four elemental energies, or the triplicity. When you need to work with those energies, you psychically "pull" on those strands.

Reach out and touch a strand in the web. It will give you information about itself. Know that if you worked with that strand, you could alter your future path, or change how you relate to the past. Now is just a time to be aware of the web, but know that you can come back to the center of the web at any time, and use it to shape your reality.

When done orienting yourself in the web, thank the web. You may feel the presence of a weaver goddess or god. Thank the weaver. Then return yourself to normal consciousness.

The Universal Body

As above, so below. As below, so above. This Principle of Correspondence is found at the heart of many magickal traditions. The human body is a map of the universal body. One is patterned after the other. By understanding the worlds within you, and the consciousness they contain, you can alter the reality of the worlds around you.

Many traditions focus on an intimate understanding of the body and its physical systems. Mystics also seek to explore the subtle bodies and subtle anatomy, along with the muscles, bones, and organs. A system from India that has become ingrained in Western magick, known as the chakras, is a great model for understanding the cosmic and the subtle bodies (figure 6).

The seven chakras are major centers of power that are viewed as existing along the spine. Each chakra corresponds to specific glands and organs within the body as well as a level of consciousness in human life. Each level of consciousness is marked by a color, and imbalances in each are characterized by certain illnesses and issues. Those centers lower on the spine are simpler and are considered by some to be crude, while those higher up on the spine are more complex and are considered more spiritual. All are necessary. Without the lower ones, the higher ones would have no foundation; but in general, our life focus starts out lower and generally ascends as we accumulate wisdom and experience.

Root Chakra (Red)

The root chakra is located at the base of the spine and is the root, or foundation, of consciousness. Here are our survival instincts and our desires for pleasure and procreation. The root level of consciousness deals with all the issues of the material world, and the struggles of life that go along with physical existence.

Belly Chakra (Orange)

The belly chakra, also known as the sacral or navel chakra, is the first center of emotional consciousness, where we reach out and build relationships with others. This chakra is associated with intimacy, trust, sexual relationships, and how we communicate basic feelings. It is also the center of creativity.

Solar Plexus Chakra (Yellow)

The solar plexus chakra is the center of power, ruling a basic fight-or-flight response. Here are the issues of self-image, self-esteem, and the loss of power, creating fear and anger. This chakra is also associated with issues of control—how we control ourselves, how we might control others, or how we let ourselves be controlled.

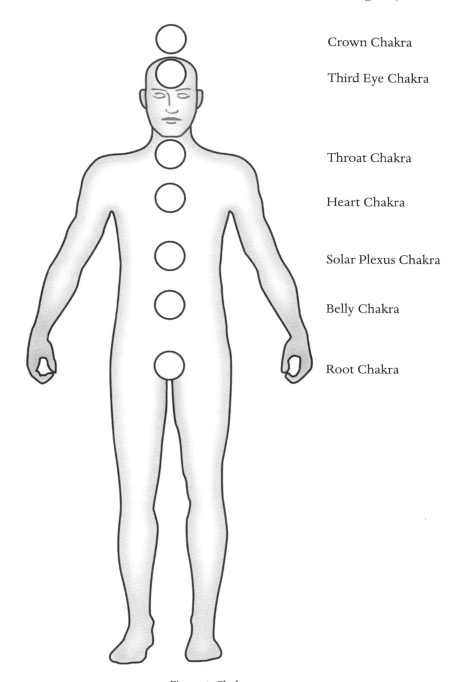

Crown Chakra

Third Eye Chakra

Throat Chakra

Heart Chakra

Solar Plexus Chakra

Belly Chakra

Root Chakra

Figure 6: Chakras

Heart Chakra (Green)

The heart chakra is the realm of love and connecting to others on an emotional level without need or control being the motivating factor. At this level we explore empathy and relationships—from family and friends, to romance, to the stirring of spiritual, unconditional love. The heart chakra is the bridge between the lower and higher chakras.

Throat Chakra (Blue)

Here is the chakra of communication and expressing your ideas. Not only is the throat chakra the energy center for speaking, it is also the power of listening, because effective communication requires both parties to speak and to listen. Here we express the will of our lower chakras, giving word and form to things that are often seen as intangible. Our expressed will is the power of the magick word.

Third Eye Chakra (Indigo/Purple)

The third eye chakra, or brow chakra, is the realm of psychic sight, both seeing images of the past, present, and future and projecting magickal concepts of what you wish to create. This chakra is our image of ourselves in action and as a spiritual center, and represents transcending the dualities of the world and finding oneness.

Crown Chakra (Violet/White)

Divinity, spirituality, and connection to the source are all in the realm of the crown chakra. Described as a blinding light brighter than a million suns, or a thousand-petalled lotus, the totality of the crown chakra in many ways is beyond most human understanding. Located at the top of the head, slightly above and outside the body, this chakra is the idea of unconditional spiritual love and connection to which we aspire. It is the soul, the higher self, and our divine consciousness.

These chakras correspond to layers of the aura, known as subtle bodies, and to the corresponding universal planes, or dimensions of existence, where these bodies reside (figure 7). Various names for these seven planes exist, but the following are some simpler, nontraditional terms that I have found to be the easiest to understand, remember, and teach.

Physical Plane

The root chakra corresponds to the gross plane of matter, the physical realm, because its needs are of the physical world—caring for the physical body by getting the food, sleep, shelter, and sensation that is needed.

Etheric Plane

The etheric realm is the primal pattern upon which material reality is built; it is like the energetic structure, skeleton, or grid. The elemental planes and nature spirits are said to reside in this realm, close to the material realm, helping build it, but not a true part of the physical. Our etheric body is the first layer of the aura, often viewed as a white light

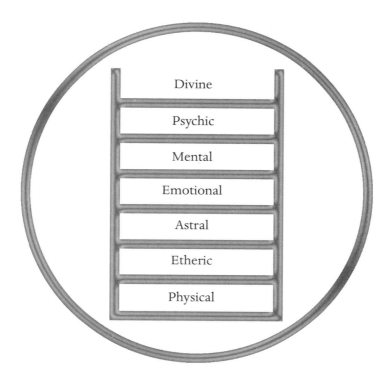

Figure 7: Planes of Existence

around the body. Breaks and injuries can be sensed in the etheric body as weaknesses and escaping energy, even if the physical body has healed.

Astral Plane

The astral realm is a more fluid and symbolic pattern of the physical. Everything physical has an astral double, but not everything astral, such as many spirits and entities, has a physical body. The astral is more malleable to our will, so our self-image is often the appearance of our astral self, not our literal image. Dreams and visions often occur on the astral level.

Emotional Plane

The emotional plane is sometimes referred to as the upper astral, containing the highest and purest of the astral plane. Here are the astral connections we build through relationships, empathy, and love. Here are the powers of higher creation, where, in order to manifest, magick requires emotion and, ideally, love.

Mental Plane

The mental plane is the realm of ideas, concepts, and design. Here is where creation is first expressed as a concept, word, or form. It is said that the clearer, more detached spirit teachers exist on the mental plane, above the more distracting realms.

Psychic Plane

The psychic plane has many alternate names, including the higher mental plane. Here is the realm of psychic energy, where divine power becomes light, the inner psychic light that connects us all. This light radiates through the planes below, and becomes the light of our visions and creations.

Divine Plane

The divine plane encompasses and permeates all things. In Hermetic magick, an axiom known as the Principle of Mentalism says: "We are all thoughts in the divine mind." We are all divine creations, made of divine energy. On this plane of existence, we are all connected, all one. Our divine bodies are all connected and understand each other implicitly, seeing the pattern of all the planes below.

You may have noticed that this model takes the simpler concept of the five elements and extends it into seven specific planes. Both models are quite similar and complementary to each other.

The easiest way to align yourself with this seven-layered system is to explore the energies of the seven chakras within your own body, which you can do through the following exercise.

Exercise 6

Rising Through the Chakras

Perform Exercise 1: Altering Consciousness to get into a meditative, altered state. Take deep, cleansing breaths, and really feel your body. Fill your lungs completely with each inhale, from the bottom of the lungs up to the top. Exhale from the top to the bottom, completely. Feel the blood pumping in your heart and through your body. Feel the currents of bioelectrical energy in your nervous system. Come into total awareness of your body.

Slowly bring your awareness down to the base of your spine. Feel the ball of red light—your root chakra—spinning like a vortex at the base of your spine, at the perineum point. Feel your body and feel your needs. Are you hungry? Thirsty? Tired? Excited? Do you want or need anything, or are you satisfied? What do you feel on the physical level? Let the red energy of the root chakra bathe you, bringing you into physical awareness and balance.

With your next inhalation, draw the energy of the root up to your belly chakra. Feel the ball of orange light slightly below your navel. Feel the etheric plane, the energetic pattern of reality. Feel the energy that supports and sustains your body. Feel your sense of trust, intimacy, and security. Let the orange energy of the belly chakra bathe you, bringing balance to your etheric body.

Inhale, and bring the energy up to your solar plexus chakra. Feel the golden-yellow vortex of power. Feel your power on the astral plane, your ability to drive forward, to bring your will into shape and form. Feel your sense of self, your astral self-image. Feel the golden light of the solar plexus chakra fill your body with power and health, transforming your astral body into your ideal self-image. Create the person you want to be.

Drawing in your breath, draw the energy up to your sternum, to your heart chakra. Feel your heart pulse with a green glow, and fill your being with a sense of empathy, love, and compassion. Feel the flow of love into every fiber of your being. Reflect on your relationships with your lovers, friends, and family, and, most importantly, on your relationship with yourself. Feel how the emotional body is the bridge between the higher and lower worlds.

With the breath, allow the sphere of light to rise from your chest to your throat chakra, transforming into a ball of brilliant blue light. Feel the light and energy infuse your mind, the mental body that permeates and encompasses all the others. Feel your mind become clearer, sharper, and more creative. Feel your power to express your every thought and feeling.

As you breathe, allow the energy to rise to your brow chakra, to the purple or indigo light of your third eye. Feel your intuitive awareness grow with the light. Feel your ability to see into the past, present, and future with clarity and insight expand. Feel your power to project your desires and be understood by the universe. Feel the psychic body absorbing and relating nonordinary information for you to use.

With one final act, draw the light and breath up to your crown chakra. Feel your connection to your higher self. Feel your awareness grow. Know that you are a part of everything, and that everything is a part of you. Become one with your higher self, if only for an instant. Feel the dazzling, blinding light of your crown chakra infuse every fiber of all your bodies with divine light. Feel the light pour out of your crown like a fountain, bathing you completely.

Allow the energy to flow down around you. Be aware of your other chakras and bodies, from the brow to the throat, down to the heart, solar plexus, belly, and root. Bring your awareness back to your breath and your physical body. Stretch as needed. Ground yourself. Return yourself to normal consciousness.

Once you are familiar with the spheres of influence in the chakras, you can use their colors and images in your instant magick.

The Music of the Spheres

The music of the spheres refers to the wheels of planetary orbit "rubbing" together, making the sublime harmony of the heavens. Enlightened sages and mystics are said to hear the music of the spheres.

Planetary correspondences are one way of organizing magickal ideas. In astrology, each planet is associated with an aspect of life. Each is named after a godform that is also linked to that function of life. Venus is the goddess of love and the planet of love. The planets are synchronously named after the godform that is most appropriate. Some people believe that the "new" outer planets—Uranus, Neptune, and Pluto—received their final names only when the archetypically appropriate names were chosen. Uranus was originally called the Star of George, but the name was not universally accepted, and the planet was not officially named until Uranus was proposed.

Each planet is associated with particular zodiac signs, colors, numbers, symbols, herbs, oils, incenses, and stones. These correspondences are used to create magickal rituals and spells that will resonate with the energy, the vibration, of the planet. By mixing several different planetary energies, you can create your own magickal symphony.

More importantly, each planet is the physical representation of a level of consciousness. If the solar system were imagined to be an entity unto itself, the planets would be the organs, or chakras, within its body. As the ancients knew, the patterns of the planets are reflected in our own consciousness: "As above, so below." The level of consciousness that each planet embodies is found within our own consciousness. Planetary rituals help us tap in to those levels of consciousness and reveal their gifts.

Sun ☉

The Sun rules primal energy and the life force. It is the "heart" of our solar system and the engine of our magick. Solar spells are done for health, vitality, energy, success, creativity, and prosperity.

Moon ☽

The Moon embodies our emotional consciousness, intuition, and psychic ability. Spells involving the tides of the moon, feminine mysteries, divination, and emotional healing are ruled by the Moon.

Mercury ☿

Mercury relates to our mind and memory. Magick involving the mental faculties, including communication, logic, and travel, are ruled by Mercury. The archetypes of Mercury are messengers and magicians, so the travel of ideas, people, and energy is also ruled by this planet.

Venus ♀

Venus is the power of attraction and personal love. Venus rules our ability to attract the people and resources we need, as well as to develop personal, affectionate relationships.

Mars ♂

Mars energy directs the will. It represents the power of pure force and the drive to move forward. Mars can be perceived as anger, passion, or drive, depending on the expression. All magick involving direct action, power, protection, destruction, or warrior energy involves the red planet's energy.

Jupiter ♃

Jupiter is the power of the higher self, expressed as wisdom and expansion. Some people experience it as grace, prosperity, or good luck.

Jupiter energy expands and is used both in money magick and in finding spiritual purpose and knowledge.

Saturn ♄

Saturn is Jupiter's energetic complement, involving contraction instead of expansion. Saturn limits, binds, and protects. It is the force of karma, the consequences of our past actions. Magick involving protection, slowing down, or time is ruled by Saturn.

Uranus ♅

Uranus breaks through limitations and boundaries. It is the power of the innovative, inspired mind. Uranus represents the higher, divine mind, personal expression, and higher ideals. Uranus energy is like a bolt of lightning or Promethean awareness, granting new insight.

Neptune ♆

Neptune is the power of unconditional love, romance, and creativity. As Uranus is the higher mind, Neptune plays the role of the higher heart. Neptune rules the dream worlds and creativity, from the realm of the artist, musician, and dancer to that of the shaman and mystic.

Pluto ♇

Pluto is the power of transformation. This energy often destroys first in order to make room to rebuild, being named after the god of death and the underworld. Every kind of death is a rebirth, a transformation, though the process can be difficult. Pluto energy destroys that which doesn't serve to bring you to a level of greater awareness and understanding.

To work with planetary energies, you should first make a spiritual connection to each planet. The following exercise will help you rise through each of these levels of energy and understand them through personal experience.

Exercise 7

Rising Through the Planetary Spheres

Perform Exercise 1: Altering Consciousness to get into a meditative, altered state. Imagine a pentagram in each of the four directions around you, charged to protect you from any unwanted energies or influences. Feel your energy and awareness expand into the area around you. Be aware of the room you are in, the building or landscape that surrounds you. Feel the gravity of the world anchor your body in place, as you prepare to ascend through the planetary planes.

Gently feel yourself rise from this place and time, ascending upward. Below you, your body glows like a star, a star that only you can see, that will always guide you back, without fail (figure 8). As

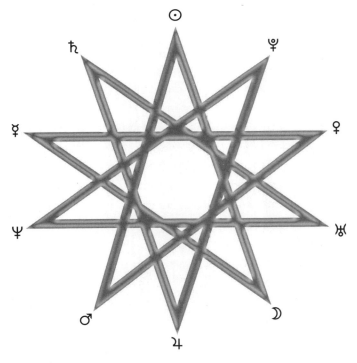

Figure 8: Ten-Pointed Star with Planetary Symbols

you rise up through the sky, through the clouds, enter the orbit of the Moon around the Earth. Find the Moon and go toward it. Feel as though the orb of light is a gateway for you to enter its consciousness. Enter lunar consciousness. Feel yourself surrounded by purple and silver light. Feel your intuition and emotions come to life in this sphere. Feel the Moon and its vibration. Feel the night and the energy of the Goddess all around you. These are the qualities of Luna.

Rise through the Moon's power and reach to the Sun. Feel the golden-yellow light of the Sun fill you with power, illumination, and vitality. Surround yourself with the solar gold. Feel yourself aligning with the solar fires, the center of the solar system, with power and gravity. You are healthy, vital, successful, inspired. These are the powers of the solar sphere.

Rise up through the Sun and feel yourself penetrating a level of orange energy. Enter the plane of Mercury. Mercury is the sphere of the mind, intellect, logic, and memory. Everything is sharp, fast, and active here. Everything races. Everything is made from language. Feel your mental abilities sharpen. These are the gifts of Mercury.

Rise up through this sphere and enter a green world, the world of Venus. Venus can feel like a primordial ocean, or a lush forest or jungle. Venus is the power of life and the attraction of energies that create life. Venus feels magnetic and heavy at times, but also vibrant and vital. The vibration of Venus at its highest level is attraction and love. Working with these powers is the role of Venus.

Rise up through the energy of Venus and meet its complement, the red sphere of Mars. Mars is the sphere of dynamic action, energy, and will. Mars is stimulating, calling you to action. Mars can be militaristic or sexual. The red energy surrounding you is vital life force and primal passion. Feel these qualities of Mars.

Rise up through this red sphere and enter the blue and purple tranquility of Jupiter. Jupiter is the power of peace, expansion, and spirituality. Feel the shift into a stable sense of power, of knowing. Feel your connection to the divine world. Jupiter is associated with sky kings. Feel the power of the tranquil sky. Jupiter is the sphere of teachers and divine wisdom. Feel your connection to this wisdom. Feel the gifts of Jupiter.

Gently rise up from the sphere of Jupiter into the inky blackness of Saturn. You might feel a stronger sense of gravity here than anywhere else. Saturn can feel repressive, restrictive, or binding. You are like a lump of coal in a mountain, under pressure and waiting to be fused into a diamond. Feel the darkness, but move through your fears, into a quiet surrender to the divine creative process. Trust. Feel protected by the process. These are the lessons of Saturn.

Emerge from the darkness into the electric-blue light of Uranus. Uranus is bright, flashing, and innovative, decorated with lightning bolts of inspiration. Things seem doubly bright after the darkness of Saturn. Here in Uranus, all ideas and forms of expression are possible. You are free to be yourself and to express your higher will. These are the qualities of Uranus.

Transcend the dazzle of Uranus and rise into the sea-green sphere of Neptune, the foggy mist. Neptune is the fog of illusion, delusion, and, ultimately, unconditional love. It is like the collective consciousness, containing both the best and worst we have to offer. Feel the source of creative inspiration well within you, looking for an avenue through which to be released and expressed.

Rise into the realm of Pluto, which may suddenly feel like a descent into the underworld. The color dominating this sphere is a dark scarlet. There is a heaviness in the air not unlike that of Saturn, but tinged with the vitality of Mars as well. There is power here, but also death and transformation. Pluto's realm can feel as if someone were dancing on your grave. Pluto is the ability to surrender to divine will, and when you do, to be reborn like the phoenix. Feel yourself alight with the transforming flame of Pluto.

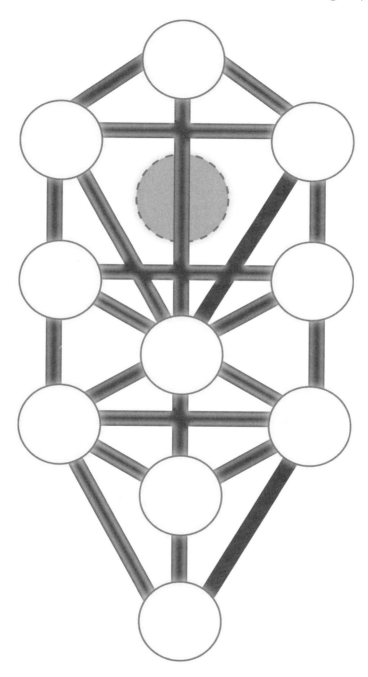

Figure 9: Tree of Life

Like the phoenix, the fiery bird of spirit, rise above the sphere of Pluto. Feel your power, and follow your trail back to the glowing star of your body. Descend quickly through the spheres—through scarlet, sea green, electric blue, black, blue/purple, red, green, orange, golden yellow, and silver/purple—and back through the sky of the Earth, back to your body. Feel yourself become integrated with your body. Return yourself to normal consciousness.

These are only a few of the magickal paradigms. Though you may think they seem very different, you can relate them together. The elements can be seen in the chakras, and the chakras in the planets. Astrology brings them all together, using gender, archetype, element, and triplicity with the planets and colors.

One of the most complex yet most rewarding magickal paradigms is the Tree of Life (figure 9). Found originally in Hebrew forms of mysticism, or adopted in the traditions of Hermetic magicians, the Tree creates a model of reality that incorporates many of these paradigms within it, from the elements to the obvious tree symbols. Each of the Tree's ten spheres is associated with a planet or heavenly body, and the connection paths have their own correspondences as well, including tarot cards and letters of the Hebrew alphabet. Knowledge of these correspondences is used to create magick, meditation, and ritual. The Tree of Life is too vast a topic to include in detail in this book, but if you are familiar with it, you can adapt its teachings to the practice of instant magick.

By looking at many magickal models, an aspiring magician or witch can realize that all are right and all are wrong simultaneously. Reality cannot be summed up by any one symbol, but each one is an accurate way to describe reality for that particular tradition. Building a relationship with your paradigm—or perhaps with many paradigms—is the first step in harnessing the energies of magick to create change.

chapter four

Instant Magick Spells

Here is the heart of the book—the spells. Most people buy magick books for the spells, and as with any other book, you can use these spells as rotes, as pre-made formulas.

Many people think of spells as scientific formulas. Once concocted, they will always work, for anyone. But magick doesn't work that way. It takes a personal connection to the forces of the universe to make magick work. No matter how perfectly you execute a spell technically, if you do not have an energetic connection to the universe on some level, little will happen. Most spells are designed to help you make that energetic connection, but they are not foolproof. Unfortunately, many people think spell books are keys that allow them to have "power" without doing any of the spiritual preparation to truly make effective life changes. You could do the spells in this chapter with the same attitude, and could still have some success with them, but you would be missing the point.

Many other spell books focus strictly on techniques and tools, but the information provided in the previous chapters is intended to give you the necessary skills to make your own instant magick spells. Use the spells in this chapter as inspiration, as examples of how spells can be crafted in the various paradigms. Explore these spells to discover how you understand and perceive magick. You could try a spell, focusing on one aspect, on one paradigm, and discover it doesn't work for you. You could then try the same spell using a different technique, and get a successful result. You will then have discovered one aspect of magick that works for you, and one aspect that doesn't. That will help your future spellcrafting.

Instant Magick Trigger

An instant magick trigger allows a magickal person to access these simple instant magick spells anywhere, anytime. This trigger is somewhat like a posthypnotic suggestion, a program in our consciousness. In order to perform a successful spell, we must be in an altered state of mind, clear in our intent, and prepared to focus our energy. We can program our mind with a trigger to automatically and easily get us back into that state of mind, even if on a lighter level. Programming the trigger involves coupling a mental suggestion with a physical action, such as crossing your fingers. Performing this combination triggers a return to that state of consciousness. With the trigger, you can enter this light, altered state while driving, working, or having a conversation, and set in motion your instant magick spells.

Some triggers have inherent qualities, like subtle-energy psychic switches that can change consciousness. They are known as mudras in the Eastern traditions. The first trigger I learned—crossing the first and second fingers—I later discovered was a mudra and, according to yogis, was used to balance the electromagnetic field and manifest wishes. It's now easy to see why we associate crossing our fingers with good luck.

Other simple mudras used as triggers include making a "ring" with your first finger and thumb, or your middle finger and thumb, or even your first two fingers and thumb. What separates a trigger from a mudra is that the trigger is specifically programmed with the intention to draw you into a light meditative state.

Other triggers may not be as elegant. In Celtic myth, the Irish hero Finn MacCool sucked his thumb to gain wisdom, insight, and magick. He was mimicking his own image of when he received his gifts, when he burned his thumb while cooking the Salmon of Knowledge. When he sucked his thumb to ease the pain, he gained the Salmon's knowledge. Similar thumb-sucking images are found with the Welsh bard Taliesin. Words of power, as well as more complex phrases or hand gestures, can be used as triggers to change consciousness. I even know of one California witch who wiggles his nose, just like Samantha from the popular *Bewitched* television series, as a focus for his instant magick.

For now, I suggest you choose a simple trigger for the following exercise. Use something you can do casually, because in many situations, you will need to be subtle when using your instant magick trigger. If you are unsure what to choose, I suggest the first one I learned—crossing your first two fingers. For this exercise, do it with both hands to give you flexibility. Then later on, your trigger will be active when you cross the first two fingers of either hand. If you do it with both hands, it will deepen your connection to the altered state. The same holds true for other hand mudras, such as touching the thumb and first finger together.

Exercise 8

Programming Your Instant Trigger

Perform Exercise 1: Altering Consciousness to get into a meditative, altered state. Remain in a state of consciousness where you feel relaxed, yet focused on the task at hand. Take a few more centering breaths after your countdowns.

Physically perform your instant magick trigger. If you chose crossing your first two fingers, do that now with both hands and hold it. Silently repeat the following words to your own consciousness three times:

I program this as my instant magick trigger. With this trigger I can instantly access a light meditative state and all my magickal abilities, for the good of all, harming none.

You can end the third time with a "So mote it be," "So be it," or even "Amen," depending on what you are comfortable with. When done, release your trigger and return yourself to normal consciousness.

Ethics of Magick

You probably noticed that the program in the last exercise ended with "for the good of all, harming none." Another way to put it would be "in accordance with divine will" or even "in accordance with true will." This reflects the fact that our magick will always be most effective when it is aligned with our true will, our higher will.

Magick is a science. The energies we are raising are real and have a real effect. Our intentions govern this energy, but we must be clear in our intentions to be effective. They have an effect beyond the power of positive thinking. Other people do not need to believe in our magick, or even be aware of it, for it to work effectively. Most magick is subtle anyway, and the majority of people would not even be aware of it. If magick is an energetic power, we always have to treat it with respect, not only in our actions but in our thoughts and minds.

Practitioners of most traditions of magick believe in some type of universal self-regulating mechanism, which is not moral or judgmental. It simply brings balance through the adjustment of energies. Magick workers believe that energy returns to its source more powerful than when it left. In Wicca, this belief is called the Law of Three, which states that energy returns three times more powerful than when it left. Other traditions have similar beliefs, but without the triune measurement. In Wicca, there is only one rule or credo—the Wiccan Rede—because with this knowledge, it simply makes sense: "And let it harm none, do what you will." Though the Rede has many layers of meaning, the basic concept is that you are free to explore your will through magick, but always keep in mind the guideline of harming none. If you do no harm, no harm will return to you. Do nothing you do not wish to be done to you in return. Treat others as you wish to be treated. If you cannot love and embrace another, you don't have to, but remain neutral in your heart and mind.

Intentions such as "true will," "harm none," or "the highest good" are ways to program our magick and prevent harm when possible. But we have to believe in those phrases as much as we desire and focus on our intentions. I truly would rather have a spell fail than cause harm to myself or others. If a spell conflicts with my true will, I wish it to fail and inform me. If my desire to succeed outstrips my desire to know my true will, then I am missing the spiritual path of magick and am opening myself up to harm on a variety of levels.

Treat your magick, and your will, with respect. Remember that the first world you should seek to change is your own, and then the outer world will change in sympathy with it. Do not force your will on others without regard to the consequences. Value your personal freedom, but remember that the forces of the universe may bend but do not break, and harmful actions eventually catch up with their source.

Magick or Coincidence?

With all magick, it is easy to get discouraged if we don't experience immediate success. This is particularly true for practitioners of instant magick, as this modern, more spontaneous approach does not have the seeming authority of traditional rituals and formulas. We may start to doubt whether all the time and effort we are putting into our spells is really producing desired results.

It is even easier to chalk up our true successes to coincidence. When we intend something to happen, when we will it to happen, we are doing magick! When it actually occurs, and we don't want to claim the enormity of our own personal power and the underlying responsibility to create our own reality that goes with it, we run from it. We say to ourselves, "Oh, that would have happened anyway," "That was just a coincidence," or "I was lucky that time."

These thoughts and doubts are completely normal and healthy, and are part of the process of understanding our magickal selves. It's rare to come across people with no magickal experience who truly assume that their magick will work all the time and that it is completely real and in no way could be a delusion. If you don't have any doubts, then you either have been blessed with an amazingly magickal upbringing, an incredibly naturally open mind and intuitive understanding of magick, or you may be somewhat unbalanced. I think it's hard to live in the rational world with traditional material responsibilities and not have such commonsense thoughts. But what you do with those thoughts is what defines a witch, mage, and mystic. If you let these doubts prevent you from experiencing your spirituality and psychic ability, you will never fully live a magickal life.

If you persevere on the magickal path, open to the experience, you will soon realize that you are consistently "beating" the odds and going beyond what could be attributed to chance, luck, or coincidence. Then you will begin to truly understand how magick works in life, and how much personal empowerment it gives, as well as how much responsibility you hold for using it. You will become responsible for all your thoughts, words, and deeds, because you will recognize that all are triggers for magickal change.

Instant Magick Spells

The following is a compendium of instant magick spells that have worked for me and my family, friends, covenmates, and students. I share them with you here to show you the wide range of results you can get from instant magick, and also the variety of ways in which you can execute an intention.

Each spell has a list of correspondences associated with it. These differ from the traditional correspondences because they are not herbs, stones, or other typical associations. Here we have the more energetic correspondences, including colors, elements, planets, spiritual entities, and words of power/affirmations. When executing these spells, you do not have to use all the correspondences. Pick the ones that resonate for you. If you work well with elemental energy but have no connection with the planets, don't try to draw upon the planetary paradigm to work your magick. Stick with the elemental associations. Be creative. For example, the Wheel of Fortune spell is prosperity magick based on Jupiter energy and the imagery of the Wheel of Fortune tarot card. If those symbols don't work for you, know that the element of earth is also about abundance and prosperity. Call upon your connection to the earth element, explored in Exercise 3: Elemental Connection and Balance, to help you create the flow of fortune you need. I have also included correspondences to a variety of beings, including animal, plant, and stone spirits.

To learn more about adapting these spells, and how to work with various correspondence systems and the spirits associated with them, look to chapter 5 and the appendix. I suggest that you read the entire book before attempting any spells in this chapter, so you have a complete idea of the system and how to work with it for your highest good.

Each spell has instructions as to how it was cast in the past, but you are not limited to those methods. These are now your instant magick spells. Feel free to adapt and change them as needed.

Alarm Clock

Intention: To wake up on time without an external alarm.

Colors: Black, white, gray, yellow.

Triplicities: Mutable, cardinal.

Elements: Earth, fire.

Chakra: Root.

Planets: Saturn, Sun.

Entities: Any deities associated with time, sleep, or dreams, such as Chronos, Hypnos, Morpheus, Phoebetor, and Phantasus. Also gods associated with the Sun and dawn, including Ra, Horus, Sekhmet, Bast, Shamash, Helios, Apollo, Balder, Bel, Lugh, and Amaterasu. Archangels Raphael and Michael. Rooster animal spirit. Morning Glory plant spirit. Citrine stone spirit.

Words: Tomorrow, I will wake up at XX:XX AM/PM. So mote it be.

Description: Use this instant spell to set your internal alarm clock, your body's physical rhythms, to get up on time. I don't use it every day, but when I do, it works! I dislike getting up early and usually work late. I hate the sound of alarm clocks and worry about waking up on time when I need to get to an appointment or catch a plane.

When I need to wake up at a specific time, I use this spell. I lie in bed and get into my meditative state. I feel my physical body and its rhythms. Then I visualize an alarm clock, traditional or digital, set at the time I desire to awake. I say my affirmation three times, specifying the time. I make sure I specify AM or PM, and that it is tomorrow for which I am setting my alarm clock. Then I go to sleep and let my body and inner consciousness wake me up on time. If you are not sure this will work, feel free to set your physical alarm clock a few minutes later, just to make sure you wake up. Once you have had success with this technique, your confidence in it will grow and you will no longer need a backup.

Animal Communication

Intention: To send and receive information between you and an animal, usually a domesticated one.

Colors: Blue, brown.

Triplicity: Mutable.

Elements: Air, earth.

Chakras: Belly, throat.

Planets: Mercury, Earth, Moon.

Entities: Many deities are associated with specific animal allies, while others are patrons of the entire animal kingdom. Suitable gods for this spell include Artemis, Diana, Cybele, Hecate, Athena, Bast, Sekhmet, Inanna, Rhiannon, Freyja, Frigga, Ceridwen, Pan, Poseidon, Faunus, Mercury, Hermes, Anubis, Thor, Odin, Freyr, and Indra. Raphael, the archangel of communication. Saint Francis of Assisi, the patron saint of animals. The spirit of the particular animal with whom you wish to communicate. Lapis and Turquoise stone spirits. Catnip plant spirit.

Words: I hear and speak the wisdom of the animal world.

Description: Mages, witches, and shamans are known for their link to the animal world, being able to empathize and communicate with animals. Through this spell, you can learn how to communicate with both domesticated animals and those you might encounter out in nature.

While holding your trigger, take a few deep breaths and focus your attention on the animal in question. Imagine a link of blue light connecting the two of you. The connecting line can be through the air or through the land beneath you. It is important not to think of the connection as too projective or threatening, but rather as a soft and steady connection to the animal.

Imagine this as your "phone" line, translating your communications back and forth. Think your message in words, or better yet, in pictures. Allow the response to come to you. It, too, might be in words or pictures. Animals, particularly wild ones, don't recognize the words we use, but our psyches are able to translate the messages in ways we all understand. I've had full-fledged conversations with insects as well as four-legged friends.

When done, say farewell and imagine the energetic link dissolving away harmlessly.

Astral Wind

Intention: To cleanse, heal.

Colors: Blue, white.

Triplicity: Cardinal.

Element: Air.

Chakra: Throat.

Planets: Mercury, Jupiter, Uranus.

Entities: All deities of the sky and storm, including Uranus, Zeus, Jupiter, Hera, Juno, Hecate, Amon-Ra, Nuit, Shu, Enlil, Inanna, Marduk, Indra, Shiva, Tyr, Thor, Odin, Freyja, Tarranis, Gwydion, Dagda, Nuada, and Arianrhod. Raphael is the archangel of Mercury, Tzadkiel is the archangel of Jupiter, and Uriel is often associated with Uranus. Paralda, the elemental king of air. Sky animals such as Eagle and Hawk.

Words: I summon the astral wind to cleanse and clear.

Description: I first learned this technique from a magickal healer. She would summon a current of astral energy, an astral wind, to cleanse the body or to cleanse a space. Since that session, I have tried it my-self with wonderful results.

The effect is very easy to accomplish. You are simply calling the patterns of change that are already present on the energetic planes. When I perform my trigger and attract a wind, I usually experience it as coming from behind me, and blowing all unwanted energies, ei-ther from my body or from the space around me, away and off my future path.

The astral wind is particularly effective for removing unwanted energies in the emotional and mental realms, including stress, ten-sion, anger, and the residue of emotions left from conflicts in the home or office.

Banish Illness

Intention: To remove all forces that are causing a physical illness, such as bacteria, viruses, or malignant cells.

Colors: Red, red-orange, black, white, potentially any color that suits you.

Triplicity: Mutable.

Elements: All.

Chakras: Root for physical illness, though theoretically all chakras, as the chakras closest to the afflicted body part are also part of the heal-ing process.

Planets: Mars, Saturn, Moon, Mercury.

Entities: All deities of healing and medicine, such as Sekhmet, Isis, Bast, Thoth, Anubis, Imhotep, Apollo, Asclepius, Athena, Minerva, Hermes, Mercury, Hygeia, Pan, Gaia, Rudra, Shiva, Quan Yin, Brid, Cernunnos, Bel, Dagda, Diancecht, Gwydion, Nuada, and Merlin. Raphael is the archangel of healing, known as the physician. Saint Luke, the patron saint of physicians. Our Lady of Lourdes is also known to heal bodily ills. Various herb and stone spirits, depending on the illness.

Words: *I immediately banish all illness, with ease, grace, and gentleness.*

Description: This spell is used to extract the cause of an illness from the body, much like drawing poison from a wound or bite. It may not literally remove the illness from the body, but it will remove the etheric or astral energy of bacteria, virus particles, malignant cells, parasites, poisons, or any other unwanted invader. Without their energetic imprint, the particles easily collapse and are healed by the immune system. I've even used this spell to banish excess alcohol from the body after an evening of festivities, before a hangover can occur.

Once tuned in to your body or the body of the recipient, through the use of your meditative trigger, hold the intention of finding the unwanted illness. If you are a visual person, you might perceive it as specks of dark-colored light in the body. You might literally see it with your psychic eye, or see symbolic equivalents, such as sluggish, microscopic monsters for malignant cells. You might feel or hear a discordant vibration in the overall sound of the body. However you perceive it, bring your attention to the invader. Outside of the body, create an illness magnet, a small ball of light that naturally attracts

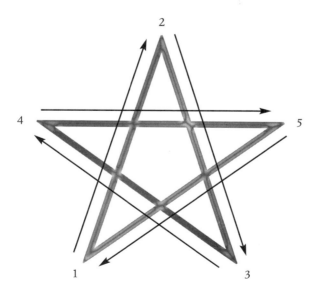

Figure 10: Banishing Pentagram

the illness. Imagine all of the particles gently flowing out of the body, through the pores, causing no damage as they exit. They gather outside of the body, around your self-created magnet.

Once you have drawn out all the particles, banish them. You can use a banishing pentagram drawn over them (figure 10), imagine them burning in fire and then scatter the ashes in the astral wind, ground them into the earth to be recycled, or send them into the heart of the sun.

You can finish the process and stimulate the immune system by using the Gaia's Fire spell (given later in this chapter) or something similar.

Clear Sky

Intention: To gain mental clarity.

Colors: Blue, white, yellow.

Triplicity: Mutable.

Element: Air.

Chakra: Throat.

Planet: Mercury.

Entities: All air and sky deities, including Uranus, Zeus, Jupiter, Hera, Juno, Hermes, Mercury, Amon-Ra, Nuit, Shu, Enlil, Inanna, Indra, Odin, Gwydion, and Arianrhod. Raphael, the archangel of Mercury and the element of air. Paralda, the elemental king of air. Ascended master Kuthumi. Stone spirits such as Amethyst, Kyanite, Lapis Lazuli, and Turquoise. Angelica and Peppermint plant spirits.

Words: *My mind is completely clear, relaxed, and peaceful.*

Description: Use this technique to gain mental clarity when your mind is running wild and racing with thoughts, preventing you from being present and focused.

With your trigger, take a few deep breaths. Imagine your mind like a stormy sky. If you are mentally agitated, it is filled with clouds. If you are emotionally agitated, it could be filled with rain, thunder, and lightning, showing the mix of mind and emotion through the symbolic mixing of air and water.

Through an internal practice of "cloud busting," focus your intention on one cloud and one cloud only. Use your will to break it apart. The unwanted thought associated with that cloud will be neutralized as well, at least for the time being. Don't focus on what the cloud represents, but the cloud image itself. If you don't see the cloud clearly because you are too scattered, know it is there, dissolving away. Work on your inner sky, one cloud at a time, focusing your mind on the task at hand, simultaneously bringing peace, clarity, and greater awareness.

Computer Alignment

Intention: To magickally improve the function of a computer or other office equipment.

Colors: Blue, white, gray, yellow.

Triplicities: Mutable to adapt to new situations; fixed to stabilize a machine once it is in working order.

Element: Air.

Chakras: Throat, third eye, solar plexus.

Planets: Mercury, Uranus.

Entities: Deities of technology and innovation, including Prometheus, Athena, Minerva, Haephastus, Vulcan, Ptah, Khnemu, Thoth, Ea, Vishvakarma, Brid, Lugh, Diancecht, Goibniu, Weiland, and Merlin. Though Raphael is the archangel of Mercury, Gabriel, archangel of the Moon, is known as the messenger. Uriel is associated with Uranus, the planet ruling innovative technology and electricity. Saint Isidore of Seville is known by some as the patron saint of computer and internet users. Ascended master Hilarion.

Words: This [name of equipment] immediately works perfectly.

Description: When I had an office job, I found myself in charge of the computer system of the small office, even though I had no computer administration experience. I was just good at figuring things out, and soon found my job encompassing computer repair along with my usual assignments. I got my reputation for being a computer whiz by using magick. When all else failed, I would use a little instant spell to get things going again. It didn't always work, but worked enough times to teach me that magick can affect everything, including technology, even if many traditionalists disagree. I started to develop a paradigm that looks at computers as extensions of the spirits of information. When treated as such, they often respond just like other spirit allies.

There is no simple way to explain this process. Each computer, system, and situation is different. Basically, using your trigger, you envision the system working properly, performing whatever function it will not currently perform. I usually shut down the system, get into a light meditative state, and then envision myself operating the machine exactly how I want it to work. Sometimes I imagine it surrounded in a blue, white, or even electric-blue light, to represent all the electrical links being made correctly. Then I wait a few more minutes, perhaps get a drink, come back, and turn it back on. Strangely enough, suddenly it works, with no explanation. I usually thank the spirit animating the computer for its hard work.

Cosmic Telephone

Intention: To contact someone psychically.

Colors: Blue, purple, orange, yellow.

Triplicity: Cardinal.

Elements: Air, spirit.

Chakras: Throat, third eye, crown.

Planet: Mercury.

Entities: Deities of communication, such as Athena, Minerva, Hermes, Mercury, Thoth, Seshat, Anubis, Ea, Nabu, Sarasvati, Agni, Ganesha, Brid, Ogma, Odin, Taliesin, and Merlin. Gabriel, the archangel messenger. Paralda, the elemental king of air. Blue Jay, Crow, and Raven animal spirits. Daffodil and Peppermint plant spirits. Kyanite, Lapis Lazuli, and Turquoise stone spirits.

Words: I am sending a message to [recipient's name].

Description: Cosmic Telephone is one of my favorite instant magick spells. I primarily use it when I have lost touch with a friend or colleague and want to contact them, but don't know how. I don't use it in place of traditional communication methods like the phone or email. We all do this trick all the time. If you have ever thought of someone and reminded yourself to contact that person, and suddenly the phone rings and it's the person you were just thinking of, then you have had a cosmic telephone synchronicity.

With your trigger held, or in a deeper meditative state, think about the recipient of your message. Say the individual's name in your mind. Visualize the person in your mind's eye. Connect in whatever way you feel is appropriate. Once you feel connected, simply think your message, usually something like "Please call me." Before you come out of your meditative state, visualize the person receiving the message. Then allow the individual to make contact.

Be sure your intention is not to force or compel the recipient to contact you. If the person has chosen consciously not to, for whatever reason, you must respect that. You can only send the suggestion, not a command, or you would be violating the ethical code most magickal practitioners follow.

Direct Communication

Intention: To enhance communication between you and another person, on all levels.

Colors: Blue, orange.

Triplicity: Mutable.

Element: Air.

Chakras: Throat, belly.

Planet: Mercury.

Entities: Deities of communication, such as Athena, Minerva, Hermes, Mercury, Thoth, Seshat, Anubis, Ea, Nabu, Sarasvati, Agni, Ganesha, Brid, Ogma, Odin, Taliesin, and Merlin. Gabriel, the archangel messenger. Paralda, the elemental king of air. Blue Jay, Crow, and Raven animal spirits. Daffodil and Peppermint plant spirits. Kyanite, Lapis Lazuli, and Turquoise stone spirits.

Words: *I am speaking and listening clearly.*

Description: Many people have difficulties in communication because they focus only on one half of the process. Some struggle to be heard, and focus so much on expressing themselves that they do not listen to the other person. Others focus so hard on listening and responding to the other person that they never express their own feelings. We often react to the other person's words, rather than digest them and respond. In the heat of the moment, we process the exchange on all the subtle levels. Communication entails our words, but also our subtle energy. As our middle selves speak, we are also exchanging information on the higher and lower realms simultaneously. This magick spell can help us more consciously process our communication.

Whenever entering into an important conversation, from a business meeting to a potential personal argument, take time to tune in to your subtle energy. Use your trigger. If the person is open to magick, you can do it together. If not, or if it's not appropriate to bring up the subject of magick and spirituality, then do so silently. I call upon my higher self and my highest guides and deities to be with me, as well as the higher self and guides of the person with whom I am communicating. Then I imagine a beam of energy connecting us—not chaining or linking us in an unhealthy way, but a temporary line of communication opening, like opening a phone line. During this conversation, I not only use my logic and reason, but also pay attention to my empathy and intuition to make my decisions and choose my words. I pause, feeling no rush, when responding, so I don't react, or worse yet, overreact. I respond to the situation. Sometimes the ideal is not met, but the process is definitely helpful.

When done, I thank and release those I have evoked, and imagine the line gently dissolving away.

Dreamwalking

Intention: Lucid dreaming, dream communication with others.

Colors: Blue, purple, white, silver.

Triplicity: Mutable.

Element: Water.

Chakras: Belly, third eye.

Planet: Moon.

Entities: Deities of dreaming, such as Morpheus, Phoebetor, Phantasus, Gaia, Selene, Isis, Osiris, Asclepius, Lilith, and Chandra. Archangel Gabriel, as the angel of the moon. The angel Asariel. Niksa, the elemental king of water. Dolphin and Lizard animal spirits. Chamomile, Juniper, St. John's Wort, and Valerian plant spirits. Moonstone stone spirit.

Words: I am dreaming consciously.

Description: Dreamwalking is an act of instant magick to do before bed, to create clear, conscious, lucid dreams. It is particularly powerful for those who have difficult and disturbing dreams, to take some measure of self-control and empowerment in the dream state.

While in bed, through the use of your trigger, consciously program yourself to awake in your dream, to realize it is a dream and to have control over it. You can repeat the affirmation and do petitions to spiritual entities, but I find that imagining myself in a place of power, or near an unusual and startling object, is a great way to "wake" my dream self. For a place of power, I imagine myself at the top of a castle tower. For an unusual object, because I rarely dream about balloons, I imagine myself holding a bunch of pink balloons because it triggers my mind to remember this strange command and know that it is a dream. Then, once in a lucid state, I can more consciously guide the dream and take control when needed. Even in situations I cannot completely control, I can use my imagination to prevent fear or potential harm. I think it's good to not banish disturbing images and scenes immediately, until you understand them, but you also don't have to react to them in fear. You can create shields around you, or become invisible, immaterial, or anything else you can imagine. It is your dream.

Deeper states of dreamwalking can occur between people with a strong emotional or psychic link. Don't enter into this process lightly, but if you feel drawn to do it, you can "send" dreams to others, giving them a message, often in much more detail than the previous Cosmic Telephone, though you run the risk of the longer message being misunderstood or garbled if the recipient is not versed in dream magick and mental clarity. Intimate groups such as covens and lodges can do dream work together, having group dreams and journeys for magick, ritual, healing, and discovery of the group identity.

Electromagnetic Protection

Intention: To protect energetically sensitive items from being damaged by electromagnetic scanning devices.

Color: White.

Triplicity: Fixed.

Elements: Fire, earth.

Chakras: Crown, third eye, root.

Planets: Saturn, Sun.

Entities: Protection deities, including Athena, Minerva, Hecate, Hera, Juno, Artemis, Diana, Zeus, Jupiter, Isis, Hathor, Anubis, Bast, Selqet, Horus, Inanna, Sin, Ninurta, Indra, Thor, Odin, Dagda, Cernunnos, Herne, Macha, Freyr, Tyr, Heimdall, and Thor. The four Archangels of the Watchtowers, particularly Michael and Uriel. Ascended master Hilarion.

Words: *These items [names of items] are completely protected from all harmful energy.*

Description: As I continue to travel and teach, I use this magick to protect any important ritual tools from the disruptive energy that is found when going through airport security screening, such as x-rays. When I travel with ritual tools, tarot cards, crystals, or flower essences, I perform this spell. Much like the Psychic Shield spell later on in this chapter, imagine the object you wish to protect encased in a sphere. This sphere can be completely opaque. You don't have to let any energy in and out as you would in the crystalline sphere of a traditional protection shield. This sphere will protect your magickal tools, preventing anything from altering the intentions you have programmed into them. When your travels are over, imagine the opaque shield dissolving away.

Filter

Intention: To keep a cleansed space purified.

Colors: White, gold, yellow, orange, red.

Triplicity: Cardinal.

Element: Fire.

Chakras: Root, belly, solar plexus.

Planets: Mars, Pluto.

Entities: Deities of purification, like Artemis, Diana, Hera, Juno, Hecate, Isis, Horus, and Bel. Michael is the archangel of fire, while Samael is the archangel of Mars. The angel Cassiel. King Djinn of the element of fire. Any totem animal spirits, but in particular Crab, Crow, Dog, Porcupine, Turtle, and Wolf. Plant spirits Aconite, Angelica, Basil, Blackberry, Cinquefoil, Lavender, Mandrake, Mugwort, Rose, Vervain, Vinca, and Yarrow. Stone spirits Fluorite, Garnet, Jasper, and Turquoise.

Words: I charge this gateway to neutralize all the unwanted, inappropriate energies of anyone who passes through it.

Description: I created this spell for when I am doing public workshops and rituals. Usually before doing any magickal work, even a simple lecture, I like to cleanse a space. I cleanse it with incense or pure visualization (see the Violet Flame spell later in this chapter). But many times I do not have the opportunity, nor would it be appropriate, to smudge each individual who enters the room. Everybody carries their own energies with them, and sometimes one person can imbalance an entire group, maybe someone having a bad day who cannot put that energy aside for the event at hand, or a person with an attitude.

Oftentimes, cleansing the space will help a person be uplifted when they enter, but other times they bring that energy into the space and there is not a lot anyone can do.

To prevent this from happening, I cleanse the space as usual, and then draw a banishing pentagram surrounded by a counterclockwise circle over each entrance to the room, tracing the entire door frame so in reality it looks more like a five-pointed star in a rectangle than a traditional pentacle. I imagine the image like a spider's web or a mesh net over the door. The web allows all balanced energy to pass through, but holds back imbalanced, harmful energy, and then absorbs and neutralizes it. I imagine a line from the bottom of the rectangle down through to the floor and into the earth, to ground unwanted energy so it will not harm anybody.

When I first did this spell, I found that in general I had much more balanced, pleasant experiences than when I didn't do it, so it became a standard part of my space preparation. Long-time students even commented on feeling something different than usual.

This technique doesn't necessarily solve any long-term problems, but provides a stable environment for my presentations and rituals. I use it in my office and even my home when having a social gathering. I've found no need to banish and dismantle the construct, as it will eventually fade, usually by the end of the evening.

Gaia's Fire

Intention: Physical healing.

Colors: Green, blue.

Triplicities: All.

Element: Earth.

Chakras: Root, but potentially all chakras.

Planet: Earth.

Entities: Gaia (Mother Earth) and all deities that embody the earth, such as Demeter, Ceres, Cybele, Tellus Mater, Isis, Inanna, Freyja, Modron, and Danu.

Words: *I am completely healthy.*

Description: Gaia's Fire is a spell used to heal the body and reduce pain. It is particularly useful immediately after minor injuries or flare-ups of older injuries. Working with earth energy, of both the element and the planet, it taps in to the primal renewing energy of the planet that resonates with our physical bodies. The healing energy manifests as a green flame engulfing the body, "burning" away all injury, returning your body to its primal, vibrant pattern. It helps to have a strong relationship with the Earth Goddess and to do this spell with her permission and blessing.

Sit in a comfortable position, ideally with either the soles of your feet or the base of your spine on the ground. Contact with the ground stimulates the connection to earth energy. Even if you are indoors or on an upper floor, this position still facilitates the connection.

Enter into a meditative state. Create a link from your body down into the earth, like dropping an anchor. Imagine it connecting deep into the planet. Feel this line of energy act like a straw, and draw up the healing energies of the planet. As it enters your body, it ignites as green fire. The fire dissolves away your illnesses and injuries. The energy physically rejuvenates you. Feel the fire flow through your body and escape through the skin as it ignites. You are releasing energy as you draw up more. The exchange releases the energy of pain and injury and stimulates rapid healing.

Do this for at least two minutes. You can hold it as long as you can concentrate and your intuition guides you. It doesn't take long to make a lasting effect. I normally do no more than ten minutes. When you are done, stop drawing up the energy. Thank Mother Earth. Let the remaining energy within you burn. Count up from your meditative state, and ground as needed. Notice the healing change in your body.

You can do this spell for others when they desire to be healthy and give you permission to do so. If possible, guide them through it as a meditation. If not, have them repeat the affirmation while you move the energy.

Golden Thread

Intention: To find a lost object.

Colors: Gold—any color will actually work, though gold and green are the traditional colors of attraction.

Triplicity: Mutable.

Elements: Water, earth.

Chakra: Heart.

Planet: Venus.

Entities: Deities of attraction, such as Aphrodite, Venus, Isis, Hathor, Inanna, Ishtar, Astarte, Freyja, and Branwen. Haniel, the archangel of Venus. Saint Anthony of Padua, the patron saint of lost objects. Animal spirits Eagle, Hawk, and Falcon, for keen eyesight and the ability to see things from above.

Words: I immediately locate [name of object].

Description: This spell was first taught to me by a traditional witch. Since then I've used it to find things that I've misplaced. While using your trigger, imagine the missing object tied with a gold thread. Imagine the other end of the gold thread in your hand. "Pull" on the psychic thread and visualize the object coming to you. Then go looking for your lost item. One parent told me that this technique also works for lost children.

Grounding

Intention: To bring personal energy and focus to the material world.

Colors: Earth tones—black, brown, tan, rust.

Triplicity: Fixed.

Element: Earth.

Chakra: Root.

Planets: Earth, Saturn.

Entities: Earth deities, such as Gaia, Tellus Mater, Cybele, Demeter, Ceres, Persephone, Proserpina, Chronos, Saturn, Pan, Seb, Osiris, Ea, Enlil, Dumuzi, Inanna, Nerthus, Freyja, Freyr, Cernunnos, Modron, and Danu. Earth elementals, including Ghob, the king of earth elementals. Sandalphon, archangel of the earth. Snake and Turtle animal spirits. Dandelion plant spirit and Garnet and Malachite stone spirits.

Words: *I am fully grounded. I am fully present.*

Description: "Grounding" simply means anchoring yourself to the physical, earthy plane. When we meditate and journey, we are naturally ungrounded and have to bring our awareness back to the real world in order to function. Participating in high-energy rituals, such as the magick circle, can cause us to become ungrounded. The circle exists between the worlds and focuses the participants' attention between the worlds. The energy of the ritual can charge the participants, and part of the grounding process is to release excess energy that is not appropriate for material-world functioning into the land. This is also called grounding or "earthing" the energy. It allows the practitioner to come back to the world more easily. Oftentimes, eating or drinking something, like the traditional cakes and ale, can ground a person. When you are digesting something, your energy is concentrated on the physical process and can bring you back to the physical world. Ungrounding also occurs involuntarily during shock and trauma. The person's energy and spirit find the body too uncomfortable or even painful to be in, and partially leave the body, creating a state of ungroundedness. People who are more naturally ungrounded are often described as flighty, and need these techniques when they have to focus on material concerns.

Grounding is more of a basic life skill than an instant magick spell, but when framed in terms of a spell, it can be more effective for some people. If you have to ground yourself, it can be difficult under certain circumstances, but if you think of it like all other acts of magick, all other shifts of consciousness, and evoke the powers of a planet, chakra, or deity, you can have greater success. When you are grounding yourself, you are automatically evoking earthy qualities within you to manifest, but if you have difficulty grounding, using the planet Saturn or the color brown as a focus can make grounding much easier. You can also apply the principles of a spell to help another person ground. Teachers of metaphysical classes are often called upon to help students ground after difficult experiences. In part, they are guiding the student's consciousness into self-grounding, but at times they are also guiding the student's energy to ground itself without the student's awareness.

Many grounding techniques exist using the correspondences given here. Some people simply will themselves back to a state of conscious awareness. Most techniques include body movement, to bring the body back to awareness. Pressing your feet down on the ground or floor activates earth awareness. If you press down with your hands, or bend over and release excess energy, you are earthing the energy and coming back to material awareness. It is traditional to earth the energy after ritual. Some people kneel down in a reverent bowing fashion, and imagine that the energy is pouring from their hands and crown. You can imagine a beam of light descending from your root chakra into the earth, like an anchor. Some of my friends describe their grounding technique as tying down a balloon. You can visualize your legs as roots that dig deep into the earth, anchoring you like a tree or sturdy plant. Some people imagine sinking into the sand to get grounded. If all else fails, eating something will usually bring your energy back to your body.

Invisibility

Intention: To make you or someone or something else less noticeable, particularly to those you wish to avoid.

Colors: All colors, but particularly black or white.

Triplicity: Mutable.

Element: Water.

Chakras: Third eye, crown.

Planet: Neptune.

Entities: Hermes, Mercury, Hades, Gwydion, Loki, and Odin. Archangel Gabriel and Elemental King Niksa. Some of the Goetic spirits confer the gifts of invisibility, but I suggest not working with them unless you are well versed in ceremonial magick. Coyote and Fox animal spirits.

Words: *I am completely invisible to all those I wish to avoid.*

Description: Invisibility spells don't really make anyone literally invisible. They help you energetically blend in with the environment so that others take less notice of you. Think of it as a magickal camouflage spell. You can use it to prevent yourself from attracting attention when you want to maintain a low profile. When I perform this spell, while holding my instant magick trigger, I imagine a bubble of light around me, much like the sacred space of a ritual circle, but this bubble is bending the visible light waves around me, making me blend in with my surroundings. You can put out the intention of being invisible to a certain person, group, or segment of the population. I cast this invisibility ring around my car and ask to be protected from all police officers who wish to pull me over and ticket me, and I ask that this be for the highest good, harming none.

Iron Will

Intention: Perseverance in difficult situations.

Colors: Black, white, red.

Triplicity: Fixed.

Elements: Earth, fire.

Chakras: Root, solar plexus, heart, crown.

Planets: Mars, Saturn.

Entities: Any deity known for its willpower and strength, including Ares, Mars, Prometheus, Ra, Isis, Osiris, Horus, Set, Durga, Odin, Rhiannon, Pywll, Morrighan, and Lugh. Archangels Michael and Samael, King Djinn, and all fire elementals. Citrine, Garnet, and Ruby stone spirits.

Words: *I am strong. I am powerful. I am persevering.*

Description: Magick can be used to strengthen your personal will. The exploration of magick is the exploration of will, and if you apply yourself to a disciplined magickal practice, you will find your natural will strengthening. You will find yourself capable of things you never imagined of yourself, including feats of physical and mental fortitude. Many of the yogic and martial art traditions build the spiritual/magickal will through physical feats and tests. When I began my spiritual practice, I never noticed how similar the teachings of magick are to yoga, but as I continued my study of both, I noticed how my magickal training aided me in the yogic physical tests that I thought were beyond my physical capabilities. In truth, they were mental feats, not physical ones. I only had to overcome my doubts to get in touch with my power. Magick and the martial arts teach us a certain detachment. We learn that the body, mind, heart, and even will are extensions of the true self; they are the tools of the magician-warrior, things the true self owns. We are not solely our body, mind, heart, or will. We are something vast and beyond those four tools. That is why the pentacle, blade, cup, and wand are the four tools of the magician.

By tapping in to that solid warrior strength, you can persevere in difficult mental, emotional, and physical situations. In more dire situations, you can use this strength to endure pain, illness, and injury, and allow yourself to respond in a balanced way, rather than panicking. It doesn't mean you ignore the problem, but you respond in the most effective way possible, rather than reacting foolishly. We can also endure less dire situations involving family difficulties. Whenever I need to fortify myself, I use this technique.

For this spell, I imagine myself in physical, mental, emotional, and spiritual perfection, my idealized self. I often feel like I am transformed by the spiritual fires into a clear, shiny, metallic or stone being. I am solid, stable, and eternal. I identify with the solid core, the divine self, rather than the fluid wave of physical sensations, mental thoughts, feelings, and desires.

When I am done with my challenging situation, I imagine the same spiritual forces returning me to a more normal state of consciousness, and ground myself as needed.

Parking Space

Intention: To find an open parking space near the door of wherever you are going.

Colors: Blue, orange.

Triplicities: Cardinal, mutable.

Elements: Earth, air.

Chakra: Third eye.

Planets: Jupiter, Mercury.

Entities: Hermes, Mercury, Artemis, Diana, Hercules, Janus, Anubis, Thor, and Lugh.

Words: I have an open parking space exactly where I want, waiting for me when I arrive at [name of location].

Description: This is by far my favorite instant magick spell, because it was the first one I learned. The continued success of this spell under many different circumstances made me a true believer in both magick and the practicality of magick in daily life. While holding your instant trigger, visualize a parking space near the door of wherever you are going. Imagine yourself pulling your car into it, or call upon whatever powers and correspondences you choose to use to connect you to that space. You can imagine blue or orange light guiding you to the space, or visualize your connection to a spirit holding the space for you. This spell might seem silly or trivial, but magick is a practical art and can be applied in all aspects of life.

Plant Communication

Intention: To communicate with plant spirits.

Colors: Green, blue.

Triplicity: Mutable.

Elements: Earth, air.

Chakras: Belly, heart, throat.

Planets: Mercury, Venus.

Entities: Deities of nature, including Gaia, Tellus Mater, Pan, Artemis, Diana, Cybele, Hecate, Athena, Minerva, Faunus, Dionysus, Bacchus, Dumuzi, Vajrapani, Freyr, Cernunnos, Blodeuwedd, Ceridwen, and Merlin. Moss Agate stone spirit.

Words: *I am in communion with the plant world.*

Description: Echoing the magick of the earlier Animal Communication spell, Plant Communication uses the same skills, through slightly different channels, to resonate with the plant world. Herbs, flowers, and trees are all filled with consciousness, and their consciousness is willing to communicate and partner with us if we only listen. Many people believe that our knowledge of herbs has been attained through trial and error, but any spiritual herbalist from any tradition or place in the world will tell you that the plants want to be involved in our lives and will tell us their properties if we listen to them.

My first experiences with plants were quite startling. Through workshops involving plant spirits and their magickal and medicinal uses, I learned how to "communicate" with a plant, simply by getting into proximity with it, getting into a light meditative state, and having a firm intention and receptivity to its message. The Yarrow flower described to me its use as a flower essence, and though it used different words, I was able to corroborate the information in a book on flower essences. Since then I've gained lots of information on both medicine and magick from the green world. Some of the plants' teachings can be corroborated in the lore of various healing traditions, and some may be just for me and my practice.

Messages can come in words, pictures, and feelings. All are ways to commune with a plant. You can imagine colored lights encompassing you both, beams of light connecting you, or do simple rituals and evocations to connect. I've found it quite easy to just sit and meditate near a plant or tree and have its world open up to me, with no formal technique or ritual.

There is a lot of confusion and concern around exactly who is communicating. People use the words deva, faery, nature spirit, elemental, and plant spirit, sometimes synonymously. The exploration of the green world is too vast a subject to cover in this book, but this spell focuses on the living consciousness of a particular plant, what I will call its plant spirit. A plant spirit can provide information regarding its species, its medicinal and magickal uses, and its particular needs and concerns. Through this work you will know if a plant needs more water, light, or fertilizers, or is happy with its current situation. I think such communication is the first step in building a relationship with the green world. Then you can dive deeper into the esoteric information regarding the plant world.

As with any conversation, when done, thank the plant and release or reverse any techniques you used to get into communion with it, closing the space. I simply thank the plant and say good-bye.

Psychic Shield

Intention: Protection on all levels.

Colors: Crystalline white, purple, violet, deep blue.

Triplicities: All.

Elements: All.

Chakras: All, but particularly the root, solar plexus, heart, and crown.

Planets: Saturn, Mars.

Entities: Deities of protection, including Athena, Minerva, Hecate, Hera, Juno, Artemis, Diana, Zeus, Jupiter, Isis, Hathor, Anubis, Bast, Selqet, Horus, Inanna, Sin, Ninurta, Indra, Thor, Odin, Dagda, Cernunnos, Herne, Freyr, Tyr, and Heimdall. Michael, the archangel of fire, and Samael, the archangel of Mars. Angel Cassiel. King Djinn of the element of fire. Any totem animal spirits, but in particular Crab, Crow, Dog, Porcupine, Turtle, and Wolf. Plant spirits Aconite, Angelica, Basil, Blackberry, Cinquefoil, Lavender, Mandrake, Mugwort, Rose, Vervain, Vinca, and Yarrow. Stone spirits Fluorite, Garnet, Jasper, and Turquoise. Ascended masters El Moyra and Sananda.

Words: I am completely protected on all levels.

Description: Like grounding, psychic shielding is a basic life technique that we all use, consciously or unconsciously. Our energy field, our aura, creates a boundary of protection for us, our personal space. When we consciously engage the energy around us, we can create an even more effective personal protection shield.

Get into a light meditative state and be aware of the energy around you. Feel yourself encompassed by a sphere or egg shape of energy. This is your aura. Be aware of the boundary around your aura. Using your imagination and will, transform the edge of your aura into a crystalline shield of light, translucent and prismatic. Charge it with your protection mantra: "I am completely protected on all levels." Repeat as many times as you need to feel confident in your shield. This shield will block out harmful energy, and allow only what you need and want to enter. When visualized with only opaque white light, the shield can create a feeling of being closed in psychically, not allowing anything in or out. For physical dangers, it will not necessarily stop them, so don't expect to be invulnerable to physical blows. The shield can act as part of your early warning system, aiding your intuition, to help guide you out of harm's way. Reestablish the shield often to make it stronger.

Once you feel confident in making your shield, you can extend your talents to create a shield around your home, office, or car, simply by crystalizing and programming the energy around the object or location. Everything has an aura, which can be used to create a zone of psychic safety and protection.

Scrying

Intention: To psychically view the past, present, or future.

Colors: All, though blue, indigo, purple, and violet are particularly effective.

Triplicities: All, depending on where your target is—mutable would be the future, fixed would be the past, and cardinal would most likely be the present.

Element: Water.

Chakras: Belly, third eye.

Planets: Jupiter, Neptune.

Entities: Deities of fate and prophecy, such as the Norns or Moirae, Fortuna, Janus, Gaia, Apollo, Maat, Odin, and Archangels Raziel and Tzafkiel. Ascended master Hilarion. Snake animal spirit. Amethyst and Moonstone stone spirits.

Words: *I am seeing psychically into the past/present/future.*

Description: Scrying, sometimes spelled skrying, is the art of gazing to induce mystical vision. Traditionally, one scrys into a reflective surface of some sort, like a crystal ball, polished mirror, or still body of water. Scrying can also be done in wispy smoke or blazing fire, or simply by staring off into the corner of a room. While in a trance state, the shapes and reflections offer symbolic suggestions that can be interpreted, much like gazing at clouds. If you ask a yes or no question, and see a "Y" or a "+" sign, the answer is affirmative. Images reminiscent of a crown can indicate power or authority. A flower could indicate issues of love and relationship. A ship, plane, or car could indicate travel. Animals all have their own unique animal-medicine messages covered in detail in other books. Each image carries its own meaning, to be interpreted by the scryer. A knowledge of mythology, magick, alchemy, tarot, or any esoteric art expands your knowledge and ability to interpret universal symbols.

This spell is the first scrying technique I learned, and requires no tools or even the use of outer vision. Get into a meditative state, and using your will and psychic energy, create a reflective surface. When I initially learned this technique, the surface was a rectangular gem imbedded in the left hand. Later, I created a mirror out of silver liquid in front of me. The benefit of an inner scrying device is that the images can be more literal and are often clearer than the flashes and shadows from traditional tools, at least initially. You can develop strong clairvoyance skills when working with traditional scrying tools, and I often use them when scrying for others, but I often prefer the inner scrying technique to reliably answer my own personal questions.

Once you have created your inner scrying device (which you can also do in your inner temple—see chapter 6), ask whatever questions you have, and let the images take form. They will most often be symbolic and have to be interpreted, but some answers could be literal.

When done, deconstruct your scrying object, returning it back to the basic elements from which you created it. Bring yourself out of the meditative state, and ground as necessary.

Sleep

Intention: To induce restful sleep.

Colors: Blue, indigo, black.

Triplicities: Fixed, mutable.

Element: Water.

Chakra: Third eye.

Planet: Neptune.

Entities: Deities of sleep and dreams, including Hypnos, Morpheus, Phoebetor, and Phantasus. Chamomile and Valerian plant spirits.

Words: I am sleeping peacefully.

Description: Even with all my meditative training and practice, one of the biggest problems I have is falling asleep. Since sleep is something that must be surrendered to, I have a hard time letting go and relaxing my mental focus. I'm much better at it now, thanks to this spell.

While in bed and feeling restless, I simply count down to a meditative state. I make my petitions to the gods of sleep and dreams, and imagine a deep-indigo mist rising around my bed. I know the mist is empowered to bring deep, restful sleep. As it surrounds me, I imagine breathing it in. Each breath brings me to a more peaceful state, until I doze off in a deep, dark cloud of restful energy.

This technique usually works quite well. The only complaint I've had from some people is that they have difficulty waking up in the morning. This spell can be combined with the Alarm Clock spell.

Spider's Web

Intention: To create stability in chaotic environments.

Colors: White, gray.

Triplicity: Fixed.

Element: Earth.

Chakra: Root.

Planet: Saturn.

Entities: Spider Grandmother, Arachne, Athena, Minerva, and Arianrhod. Spider animal spirit.

Words: *I create order and structure in the environment around me.*

Description: I have an affinity for the magick of spiders and webs. I love
the patterns and structure of the web. Through my relationship with
my Spider totem, I learned this technique to bring structure to chaotic
situations. I don't use it often, since chaos is often needed, but if
things seem energetically out of control, particularly in large groups
such as parties, meetings, and public rituals, this spell can help even
out the energy.

Calling upon Spider spirit with my instant magick trigger, I imagine a "psychic" web being woven from the center of the room to its
edges. The web is charged with a solid, stable, fixed energy that
brings everyone to center, calms harsh emotions, and puts everyone
and everything in the proper place for the bigger picture, the bigger
pattern. The effect doesn't always last long, and if people have de-
cided to cause conflict, nothing you do can prevent that; but the spell
often creates a safe space to take a peaceful breath, clear your head,
and sort out any difficulties that have arisen.

Usually I don't deconstruct the web, but let it dissolve naturally,
much like a spider's own web.

If you don't feel an affinity to Spider, you might try to create this
effect through other means. I hope this spell inspires you to new acts
of instant magick, calling upon the individual gifts of your animal
spirit guides.

Spirit Bandage

Intention: For long-term healing; to keep healing energies flowing even
when you cannot focus on the healing.

Colors: Green, gold.

Triplicity: Mutable.

Elements: All.

Chakras: All chakras, but particularly the heart or root.

Planet: Mercury.

Entities: All deities of healing, such as Sekhmet, Isis, Bast, Thoth, Anubis, Imhotep, Apollo, Asclepius, Athena, Minerva, Hermes, Mercury, Hygeia, Pan, Gaia, Rudra, Shiva, Quan Yin, Brid, Cernunnos, Bel, Dagda, Diancecht, Gwydion, Nuada, Merlin, and Archangel Raphael. Ascended master Saint Germain.

Words: *Every moment I'm growing more and more healthy.*

Description: For this spell, I imagine myself being wrapped up in bands of healing energy, much like the bandages of a mummy. If I have an injury or affliction, I put the bandage around that specific area. If I am working on any mental/emotional/spiritual healing or an overall illness, I imagine the bandages mummifying me completely, soaking my body with healing. I find this technique particularly helpful when I'm going to bed. When I wake up, I feel much better, as if my healing ritual continued throughout the night.

Spirit Gate

Intention: To open a temporary gateway between the worlds.

Colors: Any color, though I usually use blue or purple.

Triplicity: Mutable.

Elements: It depends on the gate, but usually water works best because of its association with the west and the land of the ancestors.

Chakra: Third eye.

Planets: Jupiter, Neptune, Mercury.

Entities: Psychopomps and Guardians of the Gateways and Crossroads. Deities of the underworld, including Hermes, Mercury, Hecate, Hades, Persephone, Pluto, Proserpina, Anubis, Osiris, Hel, Morgan, and Cernunnos. Animal spirits Crow, Raven, and Ant. Plant spirits of poisonous herbs, particularly Aconite, Mandrake, and Nightshade. Obsidian and Onyx stone spirits.

Words: *I open this gate to the spirit world for the highest good.*

Description: Working with spirit gates is usually done through more complicated rituals, though you can create them effectively using instant magick. Spirit gates are created only for good reason, and are not something to be played with. Make sure you close the gate once you are finished, to prevent anything else from crossing through it.

The first time I used a spirit gate, I didn't entirely know what I was doing. I simply followed my guidance. While driving home from school one day, I saw a crow that had been hit by a car. One wing looked mangled, and it was trying to fly with its good wing, with no success. I instinctively started to pull over to try to help it, having no idea what I would actually do, but I have a connection to crows and felt I needed to do something. Before I could reach the bird, another car struck and killed it. A flashing insight from my spirit guides asked me to create a blue sphere around the body, to soothe the crow's spirit, with the intention of a gateway to send it gently from its state of pain and confusion to the peace of the realm of the dead. I did so, and immediately felt a shift in myself and the area. I then collapsed the ball of light to close the gateway.

Though I'm sure the crow's spirit would have made it to the next world without my assistance, pain and confusion could have caused it to linger in torment. I have subsequently used this technique when finding the bodies of animals that died violently, usually after being run over by a car. I've also used it when cleansing a house where spirits seem to be lingering. Persistent or malicious spirits are not so easily banished, but I've found this technique helpful in situations where the spirit is simply confused and needs help crossing over.

Sword of Truth

Intention: To know when the truth is or is not being spoken.

Colors: Blue, white.

Triplicity: Cardinal.

Element: Air.

Chakra: Throat.

Planets: Jupiter, Venus.

Entities: Deities of truth and justice, such as Artemis, Diana, Hera, Juno, Zeus, Jupiter, Apollo, Ares, Mars, Athena, Minerva, Themis, Hecate, Osiris, Isis, Horus, Maat, Anubis, Tyr, and Odin. Archangel

Raphael, angel of air, and King Paralda, ruler of the element of air. Crow animal spirit. Lapis Lazuli and Turquoise stone spirits. Ascended masters Sananda and Serapis Bey.

Words: *I speak the truth and know when the truth is being spoken to me.*

Description: We'd all like to think we know when the truth is being spoken, and ideally we do when we listen to our intuition and inner voice. There are times, though, when others can fool us, or we fool ourselves into hearing what we want to hear rather than the truth. The tool of the element of air, the blade, is often embodied in myth as the sword of truth—both the faculties of reason and the powers of justice, of higher truth. By invoking the highest powers of the element of air and the powers of truth and justice, you can have greater clarity in knowing when a communication is a truth or a falsehood, and base future decisions upon it. I've found this technique particularly helpful in business negotiations.

Through your instant trigger, call upon the powers of truth, however you embody them—the element of air, or a particular entity, color, or planet—and then visualize a blazing sword between you and the person with whom you are communicating. I imagine the sword bathed in electric-blue flames. If you are conversing via the computer, simply imagine the sword psychically between you. Divine the truth according to the brightness and darkness of the flames. When the flames are dim around the sword, the communication is somehow false, consciously or unconsciously. If the flames glow brightly, the communication is true.

When done with the exchange, thank and release the sword, mentally erasing it from the space between the two of you.

Violet Flame

Intention: To cleanse or purify a space.

Color: Violet.

Triplicity: Mutable.

Elements: Fire, spirit.

Chakra: Crown.

Planets: Jupiter, Pluto.

Entities: The ascended master known as Saint Germain, master of the seventh, or violet, ray. Tzadkiel, the archangel of Jupiter.

Words: *I call upon the violet flame to cleanse this space.*

Description: Violet-flame mythology is found more in New Age esoterics based upon Theosophy than in traditional magick, but I find this technique so powerful that I couldn't help but include it. In the Theosophical model, the divine is divided into a variety of "rays," each corresponding to a color, a purpose, and a spiritual being said once to have been human, but who ascended from the wheel of rebirth to be a spiritual teacher and master. This model is not so different from our chakra or planetary paradigm. The violet ray, or seventh ray, concerns ceremony, magick, and healing, and is headed by the modern mythic figure Saint Germain. Considering his association with alchemy and hermetics, Saint Germain is an ideal Theosophical patron for modern witches and mages. Many believe him to be the Arthurian mage Merlin, or at least one of the Merlin priest mages, in a past incarnation, before ascending in the life of the European alchemist. Saint Germain is credited with quite a number of channeled books, articles, and healing systems. Some individuals claim to be his sole earthly voice, but I have found that the ascended masters, much like all divine figures, are available to all.

The violet flame is a cleansing light, being the highest part of the color spectrum. Calling upon the violet flame, often through the mediating intelligence of Saint Germain, creates a zone of cleansing and purification, banishing all unwanted forces and entities. I envision violet flame before and after all my sessions, classes, and rituals, using it much like the traditional purification rituals of salt, water, and incense, or the ceremonial Lesser Banishing Ritual of the Pentagram. I still use these other rituals, but often back them up with the violet flame, or use only the violet flame when I'm in a rush and can't perform full rituals.

The flame, often described as red-violet with hints of silver flickering in it, starts in the center of the space and expands outward, raising the vibration of the area. Working on the same principle as high vibrational incense and oils, anything of a lower, dense, or harmful vibration must either transform or leave the space. The flame quickly dies down, leaving the space balanced and clear.

Well of Compassion

Intention: To create a flow of compassionate energy.

Colors: Green, pink, turquoise.

Triplicity: Mutable.

Element: Water.

Chakra: Heart.

Planet: Neptune.

Entities: Goddesses or gods associated with wells, healing, and/or compassion. I call upon Brid. Other possibilities include Quan Yin, Tara, Maat, Amaterasu, Shiva, Archangels Gabriel and Michael, and the ascended masters Sananda and Kuthumi.

Words: I am infinite compassion.

Description: The well of compassion is a technique I developed when I found myself becoming overwhelmed in public situations. Since then I have shared it with healers, social workers, and therapists who are versed in magick, and it has become a staple in our magickal bag of tricks.

Sometimes a situation requires you to be present, attentive, and compassionate, but on a personal level you are having difficulties because the person with whom you are interacting is too overwhelming, draining, talkative, or depressed. You can be fully protected, with your boundaries and shields in place, and not be losing energy, but your heart just isn't in it.

For this spell, as you are working with an individual or group, subtly do your instant magick trigger, and call upon a healing, compassionate deity. Visualize a well or spring in your heart overflowing with compassionate energy. Silently state your affirmation: "I am infinite compassion." Feel the universal, divine, compassionate energy flow from your heart, fill you, and spill out into the room and the people with whom you are working. It's not your personal energy, so you will not be drained. The energy is flowing through you.

Notice how your mood and attitude and the general dynamic of the situation change for the better. When you are done, simply thank the deity and allow the image of the well to fade from your heart.

Wheel of Fortune

Intention: To manifest good luck and prosperity.

Colors: Green, blue, purple.

Triplicity: Mutable.

Elements: Earth, fire.

Chakras: Heart, throat, third eye.

Planets: Jupiter, Venus.

Entities: Hermes, as a god of gambling, and other deities associated with good fortune and luck, such as Zeus, Jupiter, Saturn, Hecate, Fortuna, Isis, Lakshmi, Ganesha, Freyja, Thor, Gefion, and Danu. Angel Sachiel and Archangel Tzadkiel. Plant spirits Money Plant, Cinnamon, Cloves, and most spicy herbs. Stone spirits Amethyst, Citrine, Emerald, Purple Fluorite, Lapis Lazuli, and Malachite.

Words: I am prosperous and fortunate.

Description: The Wheel of Fortune tarot card often signifies a change of fortune, a change of probability in the cycles of life. When you get this card in a reading, it is usually interpreted as a new opportunity or turn of good luck. By using the wheel as an instant magick symbol, we can create prosperity and good luck in our lives. Magick wielders know there is no such thing as good or bad luck, or random chance. Everything occurs for a reason, but if the source of a difficulty is unclear, it can appear to be bad luck. Misfortune is often simply an energy block, and this wheel can clear energy blocks that no longer serve a higher purpose.

I have used this spell for a more immediate effect in games of chance, such as the slot machines at a casino, but never to any great winnings. It can also be used to change the general outcome and fortune when you feel like you are continually blocked, when the wheel's polarity is not spinning in your favor. Other spells can be done for a specific outcome—money, a new job, etc.—but this spell will simply turn the tides and bring you many previously unseen opportunities.

While in a light meditative state, imagine a wheel of light spinning in front of you. Like a roulette wheel, imagine it stopping in a place that symbolizes you "winning." Feel your excitement from the "game" you have just won, and as you feel the energy of your meditation, draw it into you. Imagine the wheel filled with vibrant light, and as you inhale, bring that fortunate energy into you, into your body and aura. Return yourself to a normal state of consciousness, and allow the fortunate "luck" to come into your life.

At first, this chapter reminded me too much of a sci-fi fantasy role-playing game book, with such specific spells and correspondences. And in the modern rites of magick, using both ancient and modern models and lore, there is nothing wrong with that. Our ideas of fantasy fiction are largely based upon images from our past mysticism and magick. I recently had someone not involved in magick ask me if I played a lot of the *Dungeons & Dragons* game as a kid, because my classes and correspondences seemed to be outlined in similar levels. I had a hard time explaining to this person that the idea of such levels of initiation and correspondence comes from traditions of ritual and magick across the world and across the ages. It didn't originate in a role-playing game.

In the spirit of modern magick, use whatever images and correspondences activate your magickal mind. Many modern magicians borrow from popular lore, including the stories of H. P. Lovecraft or Anne Rice, or even *Buffy the Vampire Slayer*, working with new thoughtforms into which society is directing a lot of energy. In many ways, I'm more of a traditionalist, and using such modern images in magick is not my cup of tea, but it shows that you can find your magickal inspiration anywhere. Remember that this is only a springboard for you to learn to integrate your magick into daily life. Once you understand that magick is not something you do, but something you are, you will have little need for rotes and spell books.

chapter five

Spellcrafting

Now that you have a primer of instant magick spells to inspire you, let's talk about how you can create your own spells to suit whatever your needs are at the time. Once you understand the process, you don't really have to have anything prepared in advance. You can create something in the moment to fulfill your needs.

Basic Instant Magick

Instant magick doesn't have to be complicated. You don't have to use correspondences, colors, entities, or planets. These tools outlined here are optional, and are given for those people who do not feel confident in their visualization skills. Such correspondences are to show that simple magick can be worked in many ways.

The basic concept and application of instant magick can be found in my previous book *The Inner Temple of Witchcraft: Magick, Meditation and Psychic Development.* The technique I initially learned from my teachers was to focus on what you want to create, hold your instant magick trigger, and then, in your mind's eye, with eyes open or closed, visualize the outcome of your intention. Again, focus on the goal, not on how it will manifest. Create an image of the outcome occurring and how you feel when it happens. Hold it for a few moments, or simply repeat it two or three times, and then let it go. Assume the magick will occur, and go about your business.

The only drawback to this simple technique is that if you have difficulty visualizing—creating and holding images in your mind—you might have difficulty being confident in your work. In fact, the more detailed versions of instant magick spells evolved out of my students' difficulties with visualization. By incorporating numerous correspondences, students can work with the symbols and systems that they are most suited to use, and discard the others.

Instant Magick Using Correspondences

In traditional spellcraft, I learned and now teach that although visualization is very helpful and powerful, intent is the most important thing. The rituals of folk magick work even when the practitioner does not have strong visuals. A candle spell can be done with poetry and verse. A petition spell can be done in plain words, calling upon the Goddess and God. Sympathetic magick involves ritual actions. The "image" is in the actions. Nothing needs to be visualized.

Since traditional spells can be worked with many different systems of correspondence, some of my students wanted to apply those correspondences to acts of instant magick rather than use long, complicated rituals. They would come to me and tell me how they got instant magick to work just by visualizing a color and thinking about their intention. Another student simply repeated an affirmation, and had instant success, beyond the power of suggestion. One would "talk" to the spirits of the objects, places, and people involved, and receive good results. A few others simply "said" their intention to their spirit guide or deity. I was amazed at the variety of forms instant magick can take. They don't require crisp visualization, just feeling and intent.

Creating your own spells, instant magick or otherwise, requires three basic components: creativity, knowledge, and divine inspiration. Creativity is the first step, and when you need something, your need can inspire your magick. Instant magick can address many modern facets of life, so we have to be modern and creative to adapt to the changing times. Your desire to do instant magick will stimulate you to think about spellcrafting in new ways to solve the problem at hand.

The second part of spellcrafting is knowledge or research. For instant magick, it is essential to understand the symbol systems that work best for you, even if they don't match traditional systems. What aspect of the correspondence calls to you? Do you like working with color? Elements? Planets? Notice from the previous meditations (exercises 6 and 7) how color corresponds with both elements and planets. Do you feel a direct connection to particular spirits or deities? Perhaps they can aid your magick. Do you like working with words, visualization, or the energy centers of the body? Pick the tools and mediums that work best for you, but don't be afraid to stretch your wings. The more thoroughly you understand symbols and symbol systems, and experience what works for you, the better you can craft new magick.

Study mythology, rituals, and traditional spell casting to expand your toolbox. Though we call it instant magick, there is actually quite a bit of study and research to do. If you desire to call upon an entity listed in one of the spells in chapter 4, it is probably prudent to research that entity if you know nothing about it. Without this knowledge, you might be surprised to discover whom or what you are inviting into your life. Some practitioners may consider my inclusion of the entities as irresponsible, but like older magickal texts, I think the mysteries shouldn't be explained completely in any one book. Each should leave room for your own experience and research.

The last component of spellcrafting is divine inspiration. All spells already exist. Some would say they exist in the memory of the world, in the akashic records, the spirit imprints of everything that is, was, and will be. Regular meditation, ritual, and awareness of the world can help you tap in to this divine information more easily. Ask the divine creative force—however you see it—for help when crafting your spells.

Spell Design

Any given instant magick spell can be designed and implemented in a number of ways. Any style or technique is correct, as long as it works for you. It can take a lot of experimentation to find what works best.

For example, say you are outdoors doing a ritual that includes lighting a candle. You fear you will not be able to light the candle and keep it lit if the wind blows. First, know that as powerful and wonderful as candle magick can be, the successful lighting of the flame outdoors is not crucial to the success of the spell. You could do the ritual outdoors and light the candle inside.

Or perhaps it is a wedding or handfasting ceremony, and the couple really would like a candle to be part of the ritual. Those who do not understand magickal principles might think that the wedding is doomed if the candle does not light, a sign from the gods. So it would be easier for all concerned if the wind died down a bit for the ritual. With a little bit of instant magick, this is possible.

Though there are a few ways to approach this problem, the easiest would be to stop the wind from blowing in the ritual area for the duration of the ceremony. You would not be preventing the wind from blowing at all, nor would you be altering any major weather patterns. You would simply look for a lull in the winds that coincides with your ritual.

Here are some suggestions on how to execute that intent. Realize that although these approaches are presented as separate categories, they are not mutually exclusive. You can enhance your magick by incorporating more than one technique into it. You are not stuck in any one specific paradigm or expression of magick. All work harmoniously together.

Basic Visualization

In the most basic form of instant magick, activate your trigger and imagine the duration of the ceremony without wind. Feel your elation at the end, knowing the candle flame stayed lit.

Elements

Activate your trigger and feel your connection to the element of air. Feel your will merge with the atmosphere, and gently slow and nudge the air into not blowing during the ceremony. You can also visualize the earth energy rising up and forming a barrier, blocking the wind and safely redirecting it.

Triplicity

To create a place of tranquility, the energy of the fixed, or sustaining, aspect of the triplicity is needed. In your mind's eye, imagine weaving a web of strong, solid energy around the area, creating a zone of tranquility and stability, without movement or change. You can also use the image of a ring of light, bubble, or pillar, formed from stable, fixed energy.

Planets

Start by deciding what planet is most appropriate for quieting the winds. Jupiter would be a good choice, as it is associated with peace, inner quiet, and good fortune and is named after the sky and storm king who can create or banish the clouds. With your trigger held, visualize the symbol of Jupiter (♃) in blue or purple (Jupiter's colors), and feel it expand to fill the space with blue or purple, creating a zone of Jupiterian peace. You might also pick Mercury (☿), because it can aid you in controlling the winds, or perhaps Saturn (♄), to slow and bind the winds. It all depends on your creative imagination.

Colors

Colors are strongly associated with the elements and the planets, so many of the potential colors that could be used in this situation have already been touched upon in those sections. You can also use the colors directly, without thinking about their elemental or planetary correspondences. You could visualize a bubble of blue or purple, creating a zone of stillness with the use of your trigger. Yellow, for clarity of mind, is another air color found in ritual magick. Orange, for the planet Mercury, is another possibility. When in doubt, a crystal white light can be used for almost any intention. Or you could work with the opposite element—not air, but earth—to create the zone of stillness. Deep greens, browns, and other earth tones could stem the frenzied wind and create a grounded zone where the candle will remain lit. You could create balls of energy, as you did in exercise 2, and use your will to imprint them with specific colors and intentions.

Chakras

This approach is similar to the colors technique. If blue is the appropriate color, radiating peace from the throat chakra can create a zone of tranquility. Imagine drawing energy from the earth and sky, through your chakra column (as in exercise 6), and radiating it out from your throat.

Spirits

To calm the winds, you could call upon spirits who govern the air currents. The elemental king of air, Paralda, is a good choice. You could make your silent inner petition as such: "I call upon Paralda, the king of elemental air. I ask that your mighty winds subside to tranquility for the duration of this ritual. I honor you and thank you for your kindness, for the good of all, harming none. So mote it be." Other beings include the sky deities Uranus, Zeus, Jupiter, Hera, Juno, Thor, Tarranis, and Nuit. You could also call upon Raphael, the angel of elemental air.

Words

Affirmations can not only affect your own consciousness, but have a great impact on the environment around you. There is power in a few well-chosen words said with clear, direct intent. Something as simple as "The air is still and quiet. So mote it be," repeated three, nine, or twenty-seven times in a row, can create change. Affirmations in multiples of three are very powerful and are used to connect the three selves—the conscious, psychic, and higher minds—which are synchronized when entering an altered state. Saying this or any other affirmation with your trigger makes it much more powerful.

Through this simple rundown, you have a variety of ways to implement your will and create tangible, magickal change. Combine them in a manner that suits you. I personally might combine the planetary evocation of Jupiter's energy with a spiritual petition to the god Jupiter/Zeus, and visualize the flame staying lit during the entire ceremony.

Another example of instant-magick spellcrafting could be healing a wilted plant in your window garden. Healing plants is very similar to healing people, animals, land, or anything else. By going through each of our paradigm models, we can find many ways to accomplish this goal. Remember that all of the following techniques are done in conjunction with your instant magick trigger, unless you choose to get into a deeper state of meditation to do this magick.

Basic Visualization

In your mind's eye, simply imagine the wilting plant reversing its deterioration, becoming healthy, vital, and alive.

Elements

Is there a particular nutrient that is lacking in the plant's environment? If so, physically correct the imbalance before calling upon elemental energy. Common sense is as important as magick, even more so in most cases. Don't overlook the obvious. Does the plant need more water? Is the soil healthy? Is there enough air and light? Once the practical concerns are remedied, feel a connection to the elemental energies you think are most appropriate. Earth is for physical healing and would be primary in this case, but you can repeat this process with each element. Remember the feeling and qualities of each element when you call upon it. With your will, evoke the energy of each element, and use that energy to nourish, heal, and restore the plant to a balanced, healthy state. Use your intention to direct the elemental energy into the plant.

Triplicity

To aid an ailing plant, I might choose mutable energy, because of its adaptable vibration. The third aspect of the triplicity is associated with renewal and transformation, so it feels appropriate. Keeping with our weaver imagery for the triplicity, I would imagine the tired and loose "strings" of energy connected to the lifeless plant. I would then "pull" the strings up, like a puppet, animating the plant and returning it to an upright state.

Planets

Planets associated with healing include Mercury, as the caduceus of Mercury is the modern medical symbol (figure 11). Venus has a strong association with plants. Either could be used for this work. Imagine the glyph you have chosen, in its associated color (figure 12). Project that glyph into the plant, with your intention for healing. Let its vital force animate the plant.

Colors

The obvious color for plant healing is green. If the plant flowers, and the flower is a particular color, that color will also match the plant's vibration and be beneficial in healing. Perform exercise 2 to create your ball of energy. Change it to the appropriate color for healing, and gently "feed" it to the plant, letting the plant slowly soak up its energy.

Chakras

Imagine drawing energy up from the earth through your feet and body. Then feel the energy flow out of your heart chakra, the center of growth and vitality. Radiate your loving heart energy out to the plant to revitalize it.

Spirits

Any beings associated with nature can help in plant healing. Aphrodite, besides being a goddess of love, is a goddess of nature. Flowers spring up wherever she walks. Demeter is the goddess of all growing things. She and her daughter Persephone control the seasons, according to Greek myth. The Norse pair of deities Freyja and Freyr have strong associations with nature and the green land. The Celtic Green Man is an obvious choice. Uriel is the archangel associated with the element of earth, and is an appropriate choice for the work.

Figure 11: Caduceus

Figure 12: Astrological Glyphs for Mercury and Venus

Words

An appropriate affirmation for plant healing is: "This plant is completely healthy, for the highest good, harming none. So mote it be!" Try holding the plant while repeating the statement.

In the case of such healings, you can repeat the process several times, as often as you intuitively feel is necessary. Gauge your actions based on the plant's response to your magick.

One of the foremost concerns when it comes to healing should be addressed before any of these techniques is attempted: You must seek permission of the recipient. This is vital for the ethics of healing and is stressed more in human healing spells than anything else, but all beings capable of being healed should be asked first. Sometimes a person, plant, or area of land is undergoing a great transformation through illness, and on the highest soul level does not actually want the process to be stopped or to be healed through conventional means. If that's the case, you really can't do much to heal the situation anyway, at least in the long term, until the being decides on that highest level that it's time to heal.

If you attempt a healing that goes against the recipient's higher will, you will initiate a process of energetic struggle. Magick is real energy, and the recipient must expend a certain amount of energy to return itself to the state that is most correct for it, even if that state is a state of illness. The struggle can distract the recipient from fully participating in the lessons and experiences at hand. That is why, as ethical magickal practitioners, we ask for permission first. When a person is consciously engaged in the healing process, it is much more effective, and the individual has the opportunity to explore his or her personal will and divine will in a fully conscious way.

The act of seeking "permission" from a plant might seem silly. I know I thought it was at first, but I've found that it can be quite moving. You can use the following exercise to ask healing permission of a being, though with humans it's best to attempt to obtain conscious permission first. The Animal Communication and Plant Communication spells from chapter 4 can also be used in those situations.

Exercise 9

Higher-Self Connection

Perform Exercise 1: Altering Consciousness to get into a meditative, altered state. Connect with the intended recipient of your
healing energies. For a person, say silently or out loud, "I ask to
connect to the higher self of [name of person]. So mote it be."
Repeat this three times. For a plant, you can sit by the plant
when you seek its permission, or visualize the plant. If your
plant doesn't have a name, you won't be able to call upon it by
name to connect to it as you would for a person, so use visualization and intention to make the connection. Intuitively feel
yourself connected to the plant, and ask the plant's higher spiritual self for permission to do this healing. Then listen to your intuition for a response. Is it a yes or a no, or is the answer ambiguous?
If you get a yes, proceed. If ambiguous, stop and seek permission
again later. Usually you will get a yes response. Most situations do
want to be healed and balanced. If you get a definite no, then can-
cel or postpone the healing session. Try again later, in a few days
or weeks, depending on the severity of the situation.

When done and you have your answer, simply say, "I thank
and release the higher self of [name of person]. So mote it be."
Return yourself to normal consciousness.

Use the process of working with each paradigm as outlined in this
chapter to design your own spells. When you become well versed in all
the components, it will be quite easy and intuitive. To help you out,
lists of correspondences for all the systems discussed are provided in
the appendix.

Pick a situation where magick could come in handy, and design a
spell that could transform and aid that situation. The more you do it,
the easier it will be. Use the spells from chapter 4 as inspiration.

chapter six

Advanced Instant Magick

At first glance, you might be tempted to think that instant magick spells are just cheap parlor tricks, simple momentary changes to make life easier, without any deeper significance. And at first, that might be true. When training in magick, it's best to start small and build up your little victories so that you will have confidence in your larger works.

The techniques of instant magick involve finding your inner spiritual tools, and partnering with the living energies of the world around you. Traditional ritual tools serve the purpose of attracting, harnessing, and directing the natural energies in your magick. A wand naturally resonates with the life energy of the tree that spawned it. The metal of a blade has natural properties in tune with the iron and the fire used to forge it.

Unfortunately, many people get so involved in finding the perfect tools, and not being able to do magick without their tools, that they forget the natural energies are already around them in abundance. If you can find those qualities within you, then the forces of magick will flow with you. Instant magick gives you smaller ways to tap in to those forces, ways to bring the magick into your everyday life.

There is no reason why such techniques cannot be applied to more "advanced" forms of magick and ritual. You can find yourself in situations where the appropriate tools are not available, yet still have very magickal experiences. Impromptu road trips, visits to friends and family, and even the emergencies of life have forced me, and other witches and magicians, to find different ways to tap in to our magick, ways that are not often found in our ritual books and traditional training.

Granted, most of us are coming to these experiences with a strong foundation in traditional magick, ritual, and spellcraft. We adapt and make do with what we have, and are familiar with the energies of traditional ritual magick. With that familiarity, the essence of the energies can be evoked more easily. We know the right magickal "vibration" to tune in to because we've done it many times before during more traditional rituals.

If you don't have much experience with traditional magick, this next section might be a leap for you. I suggest that you study it, but also study traditional spellcraft and ritual. Learning about the four ritual tools (the wand, blade, pentacle, and chalice) along with the cauldron, candles, incense, herbs, and stones is crucial.

Just because I advocate a tradition of inner magick and inner tools does not mean that I think the old ways are no longer relevant. The techniques of traditional spellcraft are quite wonderful, and in many situations I prefer them. I just want to demonstrate they are not the only ways. Each of us must find the magick that is perfect for us, in every moment and place. A more dogmatic traditionalist would probably not agree, and would find instant magick techniques absurd, but in the end, I always suggest that you have an open mind and find what works for you. Such things have worked for me, but have not completely replaced my traditional ceremony and craft.

Deep Meditation Magick

If being in a light meditative state induced by your trigger can create such wonderful changes in daily life, imagine how deeper states of consciousness can affect your reality. A quick, light meditative state seems to work well for quick, minor life changes. These minor acts of magick are helpful in life, but longer rituals are more suitable for making major life changes. "Like attracts like," or so the old magickal saying goes, and in this case it teaches us that a simple technique is good for creating simple changes, whereas a more involved technique might be necessary for more profound changes. Getting a parking space is wonderful, but if you are able-bodied, having to walk is not that big a deal. Not getting the parking space sometimes can help you appreciate when your magick does work, and generate a sense of gratitude.

Deeper, longer-lasting, and more profound magick is facilitated by a deeper state of consciousness. A longer period of meditation can prepare and focus the mind, aligning your will and energy, aligning your conscious, psychic, and divine minds, for the task at hand.

Through using the same techniques and focuses but while in a deeper meditative state, as facilitated by practicing exercise 1, you can initiate life changes and make more dramatic leaps. The more profound the result, the less "instant" it might be, taking longer to manifest on the spiritual planes of existence and in the physical world. No real timeline can be given for manifestation, since each situation is unique. I've heard arbitrary rules about spells taking at least three days, three weeks, or a moon cycle to manifest. I've had some pretty spectacular instant results, and waited several months for other things. Be confident in your magick, and know that if it's aligned with your true will and you executed the spell properly, it will manifest.

Inner Circle Casting

One of the primary forms of ritual in Wicca and certain traditions of ceremonial magick is creating a protective circle in which to do magick. The circle is traditionally cast around an altar, using a wand, staff, or blade to mark the boundaries. The four quarters, and their associated elements, are evoked to guard and guide the proceedings of the ritual. Energy is raised, programmed through the spell work, and released to manifest. Tools such as candles, incense, herbs, stones, and charms are part of making the magick. When done, the four quarters are dismissed and the circle released.

To cast a circle in the more meditative style of this book, your only tools will be your own will, intentions, and inner feelings of the magickal energies. It can definitely help if you are experienced in traditional circle casting, and want to apply the technique to your instant magick, particularly when you do not have access to the standard tools and altar setup.

Though it may seem controversial to some, I was blessed with teachers who stressed the idea that we have all the tools inside us. Your hand is your wand and your blade. Your heart is the cup. Your body is the pentacle. Don't let a lack of tools prevent you from doing magick and practicing your craft.

Exercise 10

Inner Magick Circle Ritual

To cast a circle, start by facing either the north or the east. Some prefer the east for the power of the rising sun and new beginnings, but I was taught to start in the north, to tap in to the natural flow of magnetic power from the North Pole. If you are doing this in the Southern Hemisphere, face the south and move counterclockwise, to be in harmony with that hemisphere's energy.

Use Exercise 1: Altering Consciousness to get into a meditative state. Though you can do this circle-casting exercise with your eyes open and actually move around and speak out loud, as you would in a traditional ritual, it might be easier to do it all mentally and silently when first trying out the technique. Intent is the most important thing. Your magickal energy will follow a strong intent. When you are comfortable with this exercise, try doing the tool-less ritual in a lighter meditative state, with eyes open, while moving around and speaking.

Ideally, you can use the Violet Flame spell (chapter 4) or something similar to cleanse the space before you create your circle. Traditionally, the space is cleansed with incense, fire, salt, water, or the besom, but with instant magick, we are using pure energy and intent.

Once in a meditative state where you are aware of energy, have cleansed the space, and are facing the appropriate direction, create a ball of light before you, at least beyond arm's reach. Traditional circles often have a diameter of nine or thirteen feet, so the ball of light could be 4.5 or 6.5 feet away from you, assuming you are located in the center of it. The light is often a prismatic white light, or electric blue or violet. Use whatever color feels most correct for you and evocative of sacred space. The color may change of its own accord as you perform this ritual.

With the power of your will, the power behind the wand, move the ball of light clockwise around you, to your right, then behind you, at the same distance, to your left and then back to its place of origin. Let the light trail, creating a ring of light around you. Pay particular attention to your back. Most people will collapse their aura in the back area, since we often don't pay attention to our back and, symbolically, to our past. A balanced magickal worker stands in the center and is aware of all directions and space.

Repeat this motion three times, as quickly or as slowly as comfortable, to create a magick circle around you. Each ring could be a different color as you draw it. Pay attention and see what the colors are teaching you. Focus on the intention of creating sacred space. Create an intention of blocking out all unwanted influences. Create an intention of moving between the worlds, creating your own miniature cosmos in which to do your magick.

Now anchor and balance the circle with the four creative forces of the elements. I will use the set of correspondences that I personally prefer, starting in the north, and using earth, fire, air, and water, respectively. Other traditions and systems use other elements for the directions. You can adapt those traditional elemental correspondences to this technique. If you are well versed in ritual, and call upon specific guardians for the four directions, such as archangels, elemental kings, or the four winds of Greek myth, feel free to adapt these quarter "calls" as well.

Bring your attention to the north. Feel the energy that is elemental earth. Traditionally, it is characterized as being cool and dry. It is solid. It is the foundation, the power of manifestation. It is your body, and the world. Feel this energy. Invite the energy of earth to your circle, to guide and protect you in this magick. Call upon the guardians and watchers of elemental earth for their help. Once you feel this presence and acknowledge it, bring your attention to the east. You don't have to turn to face the east if you don't want to. Sometimes that can be disruptive. Simply bring your mental attention to the east.

Feel the energy that is elemental fire, characterized by the qualities of warm and dry. It is energetic and dynamic. It is changing and transforming. It is passion, intensity, and the soul. Feel this power within and around you. Invite the energy of fire to your circle, to guide and protect you in this magick. Call upon the guardians and watcher spirits assigned to the element of fire for their help. Once you feel this power and acknowledge it, bring your attention to the south.

Feel the energy of elemental air within you. Air is the breath, but also the mind, intellect, and power of communication. Air is warm and moist, carrying thought and sound upon itself. Feel the element as a part of you. It is the connective force in the world. We all breathe the same air. Invite the energy of air to your circle, to guide and protect you in this magick. Call upon the guardians and watchers of air for their help. Once you feel the energy and acknowledge it, bring your attention to the west.

Feel the energy of elemental water, the waters of life and love. Water is the flowing force that we all need to survive, and is characterized by being cool and wet, loving and nurturing, yet forceful and cleansing. Feel the water that consists of your body, and the emotions that permeate your being. Invite the power of water to your circle, to guide and protect you in this magick. Call upon the guardians and the watchers of water for their help. Once you feel the element of water and acknowledge it, bring your attention to the center.

Feel the divine power. Feel the divine power within. Feel the divine power manifesting all things, on all levels. Feel the source of all, the Great Spirit. Call upon divinity to be with you in this circle, to make itself known. In many forms of magick, particularly Wicca and witchcraft, the divine would be acknowledged as both the God and Goddess. Ask in your heart and mind that all acts in this sacred circle be in accord with divine will, harming none. When you feel the connective force of the divine, you can invite any other spirits and entities that are appropriate for your intention. If you have a favorite guiding spirit, angel, ancestor, or power animal, you can invite them into the sacred space.

Any magick can be done in this space. You can do the instant magick spells and any deeper acts of meditative magick. What you will in this space will manifest, so choose wisely. You can form your magickal intention as a petition. Some practitioners read a written petition in ritual, and then usually burn the paper. Here, without ritual tools, I suggest you form your intention or affirmation and repeat it three times. I usually phrase my petition spells to start with a call to the divine. I ask for what I want, and then thank the divine, asking that it be for the highest good, harming none. You could use this format:

I, [state your name], ask in the name of the Goddess, God, and Great Spirit to be granted [state your intention]. I thank the Goddess, God, and Great Spirit for this, and ask that it be for the highest good, harming none. So mote it be.

If you don't see the divine energy as the Goddess, God, and Great Spirit, you can use whatever words are right for you, such as, "I ask in the name of the Universe . . ." Many traditions of circle casting are very conscious of the moon cycles, only doing magick to receive things when the moon is waxing, or growing in light, and doing magick to banish things when the moon is waning, or lessening in light. I generally follow this rule, but with simple acts of instant magick, I've found it doesn't matter. I can hold an intention for a parking space near the door when the moon is waning. So for some forms of more advanced, inner magick, I've found that you can do things when you feel the need to do them, even if it doesn't fit with traditional moon lore.

Spells don't have to be done in your circle. You can also choose to not do spellwork, but to meditate, commune with the gods, or celebrate the moment.

If you choose to do spells, then you must release their energy. With whatever energy you have raised in your circle, imagine sending your intent out with a burst of power. In witchcraft, this is often called a "cone of power," done by raising the arms to the sky in a sweeping motion, sending each intent outward. Traditionally, one can do three spells per circle without weakening the outcomes.

When done, don't simply wake up and walk away. You lie between worlds, and must close the gateways and space before you continue in the waking world. It is very important to close the space. If you don't, your own energy can be imbalanced, as can the energy of the environment around you.

Bring your attention to the north. Hold the intention of thanking and releasing the forces of elemental earth. Hold the intention of closing the gateway. Feel the earth energy pull back. Then move your attention to the west, moving counterclockwise to break the space down and return it to normal. Counterclockwise movement, also known as widdershins, ends the ritual.

In the west, hold the intention of thanking and releasing the power of elemental water. Hold the intention of closing the gateway. Feel the water energy recede.

Bring your attention to the south, and thank and release the power of elemental air. Hold your intention of closing the gateway. Feel the energy of air return to its source and leave your space.

Bring your attention to the east. Thank and release the power of elemental fire. Close the gateway of fire with your intention. Feel the power of fire withdraw from your circle.

In the center, thank the divine power and all spirits you have invited and acknowledged. You may not feel them recede in the same way the elements did. In Wiccan magick circles, this part of the ritual is often worded like this: "We thank all spirits of Perfect Love and Perfect Trust. Stay if you will, go if you must. Hail and farewell." Even if you cast the circle silently within your consciousness, you should still mentally thank and release all spirits you have called to your circle.

Bring your attention back to the north, and imagine tracing the circle counterclockwise around you. Move to your left, behind you, to your right, and back to the north. You can imagine the light dissolving away, or expanding out infinitely to the universe. Either will dismiss the sacred space and close the gateways between the worlds. When done, return yourself to normal consciousness and ground as necessary.

For more information on traditional ritualistic circle casting, with tools, the altar, spoken words, and physical spellcraft, refer to my book *The Outer Temple of Witchcraft: Circles, Spells and Rituals*.

Meditative Ritual at the Inner Temple

For those of you who favor traditional ritual but realize that due to circumstances it's not always possible to perform, the inner technique in exercise 10 gives you a few options. You can use all of your traditional tool techniques even when you do not have the tools in your possession.

I am a firm believer in the inner temple traditions—working with the forces and teachers of the inner planes—and much of my own teaching and writing emphasizes these traditions again in the witchcraft communities. Inner temple traditions are found in all kinds of mystical orders, not just witchcraft. The basis is finding your inner sacred space, from which all magick and ritual sacred space flows. Learning outward ritual, through tools and traditions, is one way of getting in contact with the inner sacred, and is the most traditional and well-known method in most forms of religion and mysticism. Once you have a connection to your sacred source, you can adapt the techniques and work with different methods.

The inner temple is a sacred space envisioned within you, within your sacred source. It is intimate to your connection with the universe, within you, yet connected to everyone and everything. It functions as your personal "home base" in the spiritual planes, where you can meet with the spirits of guidance, teaching, and healing. It serves as an inner magickal laboratory for the experiments of transformation. The inner temple is a place of safety, a magickal retreat to contemplate and experience the divine. It can serve as a launching pad into new territories and realities. The temple serves whatever purpose is needed in your quest for understanding and experiencing the sacred.

One experience that is not often taught in traditional magickal training is using the inner temple to create outward magickal change. Any ritual or spellcraft you do in the physical world, with your physical body, you can also do in the inner temple. If you want to do a traditional candle spell, but find yourself in a place where it isn't feasible—you're a guest in someone's home, the people around you would not understand, you don't have any candles, you're at work, etc.—you can do the spell in the inner temple.

Through meditation and inner pathworking, visit your inner temple, your inner sacred space. Your inner temple may not be a temple at all, but a place in nature. It will reflect your own spirituality, from this life and perhaps previous ones. Its structure and shape will even inform and teach you on the path. A guided meditation from my previous book *The Inner Temple of Witchcraft: Magick, Meditation and Psychic Development* is provided here if you have never experienced an inner temple meditation. This is an abbreviated version. For the full meditation, and the corresponding information, see that book.

Exercise 11

The Inner Temple

Start Exercise 1: Altering Consciousness to get into an altered state. In your mind's eye, visualize the great world tree, a gigantic tree reaching up to the heavens and deep below the earth, larger than any tree you have ever seen. It is a sacred tree, and you may recognize it as an oak, ash, pine, willow, or any other tree that has meaning for you.

Imagine that the screen of your mind's eye is like a window or doorway, a portal through which you can easily pass. Step through the screen and stand before the world tree. Look up and feel its power. Touch the tree and place in it the intention of visiting your inner temple.

Look around the base of the giant tree and at the roots, and search for a passageway. It may be a hole or tunnel or even a pool of water that gives you entry into the tree. As you enter, you find yourself in a tunnel, winding and spiraling to your inner temple.

At the end of the tunnel you see a light, and you move toward it and step out into your inner temple. Look around. Take stock of all you see. Notice all the fine details of your sacred space. Let the images come to you.

First look for a reflective surface, a mirror or pool of some kind. Gaze into the mirror and see yourself, your spiritual self, as you truly are. Look at your self-image. Do you like it? Do you like yourself? More importantly, do you love yourself? Love is the foundation of true magick. Look yourself in the eyes and tell yourself you are loved.

Leave the mirror and continue exploring, looking for your place of water. Here you bathe in the water of your own power. Think of all your worries, hopes, fears, dreams, and insecurities. Think of all the things that bring you unrest. Feel them rise out of your body and sit on the surface of your skin, and then wash them away. Wash away all that does not serve your highest good, and release it, to be dissolved in the waters.

Journey to the center of your temple, if you are not already there. Take a look around your sacred space. Feel it. Know it. Reflect upon its structure, shape, form, and color. If there is anything about your temple that you do not like, you can change it now by doing some inner spiritual decorating.

Once done, return through the world tree tunnel that brought you to this place, and stand before the world tree. Step back through the screen of your mind's eye, and let the world tree gently fade from view. Erase the image of the world tree, and return yourself to normal consciousness. Do any necessary grounding.

While at your inner temple, use your will, imagination, and visualization skills to create whatever tools you need. Remember, the wand is a focus for your will. If you are in touch with your will, you can manifest an inner wand. The blade is for truth, the chalice for compassion, and the pentacle for sovereignty. Know these qualities within you.

If you need a red candle, manifest a red candle in your inner temple. If you choose to work with a particular herb or stone, manifest it by evoking the spirit of the herb or stone. If I needed vervain for a spell while at my inner temple, I would say in my inner voice, "I, Christopher John, call upon the plant spirit of vervain to aid me in the magick. Hail and welcome." I might "find" some vervain growing in my temple, or go to my inner temple's "workroom" and find a "jar" of vervain. Perhaps I would just call a vortex of vervain energy to my inner temple, without shape and form, but pure plant spirit medicine.

Perform the ritual as you normally would, but in your mind and heart. You don't have to physically move or speak, as you might in the previous circle-casting ritual. "See" and "feel" yourself doing the ritual, even though it is your self-image, your energy body, that is really doing the ritual in your inner temple, rather than your physical body. You are still aware of your motionless body in the physical world. You are aware of both realities at once, but are focusing your attention more on the inner reality than the physical one.

Cast your circle. Evoke the elements and the gods. While in the inner temple, your vision and experience of the gods and spirits may be more direct, vivid, and dynamic. Go with it. They may provide additional energy or instructions that you wouldn't be as aware of when doing a physical ritual.

When done, complete the ritual as you normally would in the physical world. Then return your consciousness to the physical world, secure that you have raised sufficient energy to make your magick work.

It's important to realize that although I personally find this technique quite wonderful, and have used it often, it's not a permanent substitute for traditional ritual. If you never perform traditional physical rituals, perhaps because your magickal training never emphasized the outer ritual workings of magick, then this technique can help you integrate ritual with your inner magickal workings. I find that a balance of both inner and outer work, inner and physical rituals, works best in my own spiritual practice. The act of physically moving along with energy, physically speaking evocations and spells, and partnering with physical aspects of the natural world through stones and herbs is incredibly rewarding. I tend to use this inner technique when it is not feasible or practical to do an outer ritual. I don't want to discourage you from doing ritual, or encourage you to throw out traditional ritual, if it is a part of your path. I just want to share an additional technique for your magickal toolbox.

Empowering Objects

Magickal energies can be infused into physical objects. An object can serve as a focus for the energies. You can charge an object with a specific spell, or use your energy to manifest the powers of a natural object, such as a stone or herb. You can also use your energy to manifest the powers of a traditional symbol, such as a pentacle or rune. You can empower an object with an intention, and then give it away to another. You don't have to be present to have the magick work. It's a way to bridge the gap between your mundane and magickal worlds using simple tools. You can also empower an object that you will use yourself, particularly in situations where you cannot focus on your instant magick. Wearing a pentacle ring or pendant empowered for psychic protection is easier than continually doing your trigger and mentally reinforcing your shields when facing a friend or coworker who constantly drains you.

When an object is empowered for ritual use, it is called charging, consecrating, or hallowing. The object is cleansed of any unwanted energetic influence, and then imprinted with a specific or general intention. The ritual cup is imprinted with the energies of water and the

Goddess, and the blade with air and the God. Usually such objects are touched only by those who are involved in magick, and only in sacred ritual space. Many practitioners will cover them in silk until such times, fearing their power will dissipate otherwise.

Other times an object is a vessel for a specific spell—with either an end goal in sight, such as finding a lover, or a long-term, nonspecific goal, such as general protection or health. When objects are empowered with specific spells and effects, they are said to be enchanted.

Traditionally, objects to be empowered are usually made of natural substances. Though as a modern witch I have no bias against using synthetic objects, I have found that metals and stones, in particular, take an intention the best and hold it the longest. In our magickal correspondences, each metal is associated with a specific planet and power, and is particularly appropriate for specific workings, as shown in the following table.

Metal	Planet	Magickal Workings
Gold	Sun	Success, prosperity, health, creativity
Silver	Moon	Psychic ability, emotional healing, creativity
Quicksilver	Mercury	Communication, language, mental ability
Copper	Venus	Love, pleasure, money, art
Iron	Mars	Protection, success, victory
Tin	Jupiter	Prosperity, spirituality, teaching, guidance
Lead	Saturn	Protection, karmic healing, understanding life lessons

Most modern practitioners will not use the toxic liquid quicksilver. Some substitute aluminum for it, while others feel aluminum is not magickal enough. I've had great success with aluminum. Traditionally, iron is used for protection by grounding unwanted energies, like a lightning rod, so many feel it is not appropriate for non-Martian magick. Lead, likewise, is very dense and grounding, and is not used for general purposes. Lead can be hard to obtain because it is potentially poisonous, so many magicians use pewter as a substitute. My favorite all-purpose metals are gold, silver, and copper, though copper and silver usually win out due to their availability and cost when compared to gold. I like to use coins, particularly pennies and foreign coins, as my medium for metal magick, unless I have a nice piece of jewelry I can focus upon.

Stone in general is a wonderful medium, particularly those stones with a high quartz content. Most of the standing stones of Europe, renowned for their magickal abilities, have quartz within them. Quartz points, polished pieces, and other rocks with quartz content are excellent for magick. They are considered all-purpose amplifiers, in tune with the power of the world. I also like smooth beach and river stones. Other rocks and minerals have different properties, and an exploration of mineral magick can be quite rewarding.

Wood and other plant matter are other mediums for magick, and quite powerful too, though their charge is often not as long-lasting as that of minerals and metals. Candles can also be empowered to send or receive energy.

Don't limit your choices to traditional correspondences. Anything can be empowered. Clothing, hats, jewelry, appliances, stuffed animals, toys, photos, paper, pens, paintings, and food can all be vessels for magick.

The first step to empower an object is to cleanse it. Most traditions have cleansing rituals that involve salt, water, fire, and smoke, but in instant magick you can connect to cleansing energies without those rituals when needed. I hold the object and imagine filling it with cleansing, pure light—either a crystal white light or a white light tinged with violet, the highest color in the visible spectrum. I feel these intense energies, coupled by my will and intention, clear the object and leave it in a natural state, ready to be imprinted with my spell.

If you have a particularly powerful object you wish to use, or perhaps one with other strong energies already apparent, like an object passed down in your family, you might want to sit and meditate with the object. Ask the spirit of the object if it wants to be used in the way you intend, and use your intuition to determine what method would be best to cleanse and imprint it with your magick. While in a meditative state, project your mind from your inner awareness, down into the object, and consult with its spirit, its naturally accumulated wisdom and energy. (See also the section on body talking at the end of chapter 7.) You may feel that your object has not accumulated a sense of consciousness to respond to you. If so, simply meditate and ask yourself if this process is right for all concerned, and follow your intuition.

The second step is to empower the cleansed object. Think about your intention. Get into your meditative state or perform your trigger. Use the systems and tools that empower your instant magick. Connect with the appropriate energies from whatever worldviews you hold. As you hold the object, either visualize, speak, or will your specific instructions into the object. Repeat the process as many times as necessary, until you feel the intention and magick has taken hold and is completely clear to the object, and to the universe.

When done, imagine you are "fixing" the magick so it cannot be easily undone. It's like pulling the tab on a cassette, or clicking the "read only" button on a computer file, so no one can alter your magick unless they know what they are doing. Then use the object as intended.

For example, I might do a spell to help a friend of mine feel more confident in her social life. She gets nervous around people she doesn't know. Women intimidate her, and she gets tongue-tied around men to whom she is attracted. I pick a nice, shiny new penny. Once cleansed, I hold it and imagine it filling with waves of love. I imagine the love as green light, and see the penny absorb the green light and reflect and pulse with this self-love, radiating inner beauty, inner confidence, and inner light. I imagine my friend holding the penny, and see her shining with green, loving, and attractive light. She looks confident. People are responding to her pleasantly. Everything in her path is smooth because she feels comfortable with herself. I finish up by fixing my intent and giving my friend the penny. I tell her to carry it in the bottom of her purse and forget about it. Silently and slowly, it works its magick on her, and the changes I envisioned become closer and closer to reality. When she feels she no longer needs the spell, she can give me back the penny, and I can remove the enchantment by re-cleansing it. Though the spell might work for someone else, I didn't do it for someone else, so the penny might be useless to them unless I or someone else modifies it.

Location Spells

You can also empower a location. This is done through a partnership with the energy of the land and any buildings constructed upon it. Places are usually enchanted with a general, all-purpose intention rather than a specific, goal-oriented spell, though goal-oriented spells are possible.

General intentions can include creating an area of sacred space that facilitates ritual and communion between the worlds. The space can be used for ritual or meditation, but in general holds a quality that is of a "higher vibration" than other locations. Any area where rituals are frequently done will build up this vibration eventually, but performing magick to specifically create a sacred space location will speed up the process.

A healing center can be empowered to be a place of rejuvenation, peace, and insight. A business can be charged for prosperity. A reading room can be consecrated for insight and awareness, as well as receptivity, because those who receive psychic readings are not always ready to hear the messages that are appropriate for them. A garden nursery can be charged for healthy growth, while a health food store can be charged to maintain the energy of fresh, healing foods. The only limit is your imagination.

Specific spells on locations could include making a place you are selling desirable and attractive to those who would buy it. Such spells, and in fact all spells, should be removed before you sell a location. It's not fair to the new owners to have magick workings continue without their knowledge. They need to be able to imprint their own energy upon a place and mark out their own space.

You empower a location just as you do an object, except you cleanse the whole location. You consult the spirits of the land and buildings to make sure this action is agreeable to them, and then instead of holding the object, you "hold" the entire territory in your mind as you imprint and fix your intention.

The most common location spell is for protection. Such large protection spells are called wards, and the process of creating a protected space is called warding. Wards energetically and psychically protect a space. Most witches and mages I know ward their homes, vehicles, and even businesses. Such spells are done through a variety of modern and traditional rituals. Many are highly complicated and involve numerous objects and tools to make very effective, semipermanent wards. They should be reestablished every so often. I try to do so at least every year. If visiting a place for a short period of time, I will ward the hotel or guest room where I am staying with a simpler, instant-magick form of ward.

To create a ward, cleanse the area of your home and land with light. Commune with the spirits of the land, call upon your gods and guides for help, and if the warding feels right to you, then proceed. Simply hold the idea of the entire space in your mind. Call upon the forces of protection from your paradigm, from the planets to the colors or elements, that speak most strongly of protection. Perhaps, in this case, you will call upon all forces, to be protected on all levels. Imagine a shape or structure of protection around the area. It could be a bubble or shield, both of which are fairly common choices among magickal practitioners. It could also be a pyramid, crystal, castle, or mountain. All are acceptable shapes. If you work with spirits, call upon spirits of protection. Many practitioners call the totem of Wolf, Dog, Turtle, or Dragon to protect the place. Let your magickal style and persona inform you as to the form and techniques that will be most powerful for you. As you enter the realms of more "advanced" magick, the steps are not always clear-cut. You have to trust yourself and your guidance to create the personal vision that suits your own workings. When done, affirm and fix your creation, and check on it periodically to reinforce it.

These are just some of the examples of advanced magick. The key to advanced magick is to follow your own path, your own guidance, and create your own rituals, techniques, and mysteries to share with others. Let your spirit and imagination guide you. As long as your magick harms none, all things are possible.

chapter seven

Instant Healing

Out of all the magickal disciplines to learn, healing is the most important to me. Learning healing techniques proved to me how powerful and effective magick really is. Though I learned more complicated healing rituals, I always went back to the foundations of my training, the inner mental magick that you can do anywhere and at any time.

Many of my first experiences with healing involved instant magick techniques. I was very drawn to witchcraft as a healing art, looking to our history as cunning women and men with knowledge of herbs and folk remedies. I expected to learn such arts right away, as the foundation of the Craft. Though I did learn them, the first healing technique I learned was using colored light to affect health, both physical and mental. It required no tools or harvesting of herbs. I found myself using it often and effectively, for my own healing and to help those around me. Through this rebalancing, I banished headaches, colds, and pains, jump-starting the rejuvenation process within me.

Understanding, awareness, and control of the physical body are critical in deeper forms of magick. I use the techniques in this chapter not only to heal myself when feeling ill, but to maintain health by using them preventively, vastly improving my overall well-being. The simple act of taking time to meditate regularly seemed to clear many of my minor health problems, including a severe ragweed allergy. Though it is not a substitute for traditional, mainstream medical care, magickal healing has made me much less dependent upon the medical community.

If everything is made up of energy, then all illnesses are also made up of energy. If you know how to manipulate the flow of energy in your body, and you know how to conduct the flow of energy in the environment around you, into and out of you, you can make significant shifts in your energetic health. If you make a change in your energetic health, your physical health will follow suit.

Body Control

The first step to better health is learning to control yourself. Most people are not aware of the ways in which their bodies respond to their thoughts and emotions. Many common illnesses are caused by what healers call "blockages." They are energetic blockages, places where the energy of the body does not flow freely. When the energy becomes stagnant, the physical activities in that part of the body also become stagnant and eventually become a place of weakness, susceptible to illness and injury. In a holistic model of health, a practitioner helps you remove these blockages so the energy can flow freely and your body can restore itself to optimum health.

You can do a lot to remove these energetic blockages yourself, and prevent them from forming in the first place. Difficult thoughts and emotions interrupt the flow of energy in the body. When you are in a state of fear, anger, jealousy, shame, depression, worry, or stress, your consciousness contracts, creating a stress on the body. Different parts of the body—catalogued through the chakras, astrology, and a variety of esoteric healing systems—naturally correspond to certain types of thoughts and emotions. The stagnant energy from a particular thought or emotion often lodges in a specific place in the body. People with a lot of anger issues often have an energetically imbalanced liver. Those who have difficulty speaking up usually have imbalanced energy near the throat and thyroid. The body responds in ways that tell us what thoughts and feelings are adversely affecting our health. We just have to learn to listen to it.

If you can manage these thoughts and feelings on the mental and emotional planes before they become long-standing issues that develop into physical ailments, you can go a long way in becoming a healthier person. You have already learned the most important technique to improve your health—Exercise 1: Altering Consciousness (chapter 2). A regular meditation program integrated into your life gives you the time and space to work out these issues before they manifest as physical problems. I've also found regular journaling to be very effective. Once I write something down, I feel I have to act upon it. I can't just cover up the issue anymore.

When you alter your brain waves, your biorhythms and body chemistry also change. When you calm down, your body releases stress and the blockages that can cause illness. Many times the best way to treat an illness, at least in the short term, is to alter your consciousness and allow your body to repair itself. I once developed a serious cough stemming from bronchial pneumonia. I coughed nonstop, to the point that I wasn't able to breathe and my heartbeat was racing. Only when my partner reminded me of my spiritual tools was I able to induce a light trance state, stop the coughing, and eventually get to a doctor. By the time I did receive medical treatment, I was already on my way to recovery. Although it was still smart to check in with a medical professional, I was able to stave off the crisis through my magick.

Here is a variation of the meditation in exercise 1. It will teach you to control your heartbeat and metabolism.

Exercise 12
Heartbeat Control

1. Start Exercise 1: Altering Consciousness to get into your magickal mindset. Ask that this be for your highest good, harming none.

2. Feel your heartbeat, nice and relaxed, slow and steady. Feel the pulse of it move through your body. Feel and know your natural rhythm. You can physically put your hand on your chest or neck to feel your pulse better. Does this feel like the

right pace for you? Are you a little stressed, or relaxed? Pay attention to your heartbeat, and make this practice a part of your daily life.

3. With just your simple intention, imagine your heartbeat getting faster, more excited, but keeping within a normal, safe range. Imagine yourself receiving exciting news, and feel your heartbeat increase slowly. Feel the shift.

4. Then, through intention, imagine your heartbeat getting slower, more relaxed, until it is at the level of peaceful, restful sleep. Feel the slow, steady, yet relaxed heartbeat. Feel the shift from excited to peaceful through the power of your magickal will.

5. Intend that your heartbeat return to the level that is correct and good for you at this time, and notice the shift. Does it get faster or slower? Is it different from when you started the exercise? How do your body, mind, and emotions feel at this level? Relax and allow the natural process to occur.

6. Return yourself to normal consciousness, counting up and giving yourself clearance and balance. Do any necessary grounding.

This exercise is easier to do in difficult circumstances if you practice it regularly with your meditations.

Magickal Breath

Breathing exercises are a part of magick and mysticism, and can greatly improve your overall health and well-being. By shifting your breath (as in exercise 1) to relax, you change your consciousness. Different breaths, with different intentions, can be used to alter your body and awareness in many ways.

One of the most useful healing breaths I've learned is the Breath of Fire, from the kundalini yoga tradition as taught by the late Yogi Bhajan, Ph.D. Breath of Fire is said to do for your body in two minutes what an hour of normal breathing does. It raises metabolism and body temperature, burns calories, and detoxifies the body. Spiritually, it helps clear the energy bodies, particularly when combined with other exercises in this yogic tradition. Breath of Fire is the hallmark of kundalini yoga. I use it to energize myself before rituals or meditations, to free up energy and allow it to flow better during my magickal practices. I also use it to energize my mind and body, before a workshop, while driving in the car, or between exercises at the gym.

The following exercise outlines the steps of this very powerful breath. Although it may seem complicated at first glance, once you experience it, Breath of Fire is very easy to perform.

Exercise 13
Breath of Fire

1. Sit supported with your spine straight. Traditionally, you sit in easy pose, a simple cross-legged position on the floor. You can also sit in a chair, with your spine straight. Use whatever position works best for you and your body. Once you know this breath, you can do it standing up, walking, or however you want.

2. Start a rapid breath, equal on the exhale and inhale, ranging from 120 to 240 beats per minute. A musician's metronome can be helpful to find this pace. This rapid breath is powered by the belly/solar plexus point, but is not a bumping of the belly. It's relatively shallow and can almost feel like hyperventilating. If you begin to feel that way, slow down the breath and work your way up to the traditional speeds. The chest is lifted and stays still. The spine doesn't flex.

3. Once you have the rapid breath going, repeat silently in your mind the mantra "Sat" on the inhale and "Nam" on the exhale. Sat Nam means "true name" and refers to your divine self, soul, or higher self. The mantra helps elevate your consciousness while you do the breath.

4. Try Breath of Fire only for two minutes to start, if you can. You can work up to longer periods of time, though most

yogic-exercise sets recommend performing it for two to five minutes at a time.

5. Kundalini yogis often end Breath of Fire exercises with what is called the root lock, or mulbandh. It locks the energy released during the breath in the body's energy systems, preventing it from dissipating from the body, and allows that energy to circulate up and down the spine. Inhale fully and contract your rectum and sex organ. Squeeze your navel back to your spine. Hold your breath for three to five seconds, and then exhale fully.

6. Return to normal breathing, and rest for a minute.

You don't have to end with the root lock. Breath of Fire works fine without it. The lock just gives it an extra bit of power.

A second kundalini-yoga exercise I enjoy is a cooling breath known as Sitalee Pranayam. This meditative breath cools you down, calms your nerves, sheds stress, and develops your meditative mind.

Exercise 14

Cooling Breath

1. Sit in a comfortable, easy pose, spine straight and supported, as in Exercise 13: Breath of Fire.

2. Extend your tongue slightly past your teeth and lips.

3. Curl your tongue into a U shape. Some people physically cannot do this, and that's fine. The breath will still work. But if you can, try to form the curled U shape.

4. Inhale through your tongue to allow the air to hit the center of the tongue as it moves into the chest. Breathe deeply. This breath isn't fast, like Breath of Fire.

5. Retract your tongue, close your lips, and exhale smoothly through your nose, as completely as you can, pulling your navel back to your spine to completely empty your lungs.

6. With your eyes still closed, direct your eyes toward the brow, focusing your attention on the third eye chakra. Keep your

eyes closed and directed toward the brow while you breathe in and out.

7. You can also use the Sat Nam mantra—"Sat" on the inhale and "Nam" on the exhale.

8. Do this breath for two minutes. When done, inhale, hold for a few seconds, and release. Breathe normally and rest.

Polarity breathing is another technique I learned in my initial magickal training. Technically, polarity breathing is composed of two different exercises—positive breathing and negative breathing—that are used to establish an energetic balance. This technique was originally found in *Wisdom of the Mystic Masters* by Joseph J. Weed. Though I usually do not use the terms positive and negative to denote good and bad, I love these exercises. I prefer to use the terms positive and negative to refer to electrical charges, and if I want to banish harm, illness, or danger, rather than say "I banish all negative energy," I say that I banish the harmful energy, illness, or dangerous forces.

Use the positive breathing exercise to counterbalance "a negative condition." I was taught to use it when feeling out of sorts, depressed, or downtrodden. It returns a sense of balance and even optimism, neutralizing the negative energy. You can repeat this process in chronic situations, but you should wait for two hours between sessions.

Exercise 15

Positive Breathing

1. Sit in a comfortable position, with your hands in your lap and your feet squarely on the floor, without touching each other.

2. Take a few deep breaths to prepare for the meditation.

3. Touch the index finger, middle finger, and thumb of one hand to the corresponding fingers on the other hand, forming a triangle.

4. Take a deep breath, and hold it for a count of seven. Exhale.

5. Repeat step 4 six more times.

6. Release your hands and breathe normally. Put the whole exercise out of your mind, and let your energy naturally return to balance.

Negative breathing is said to counteract an "overpositive" condition, when a person has too much energy and is frantic or nervous. It is especially helpful for someone suffering from the early stages of the common cold. If done soon enough, this breath helps remove the germs that cause the cold in six to eight hours.

Exercise 16

Negative Breathing

1. Sit in a comfortable position, with your hands in your lap and your feet squarely on the floor. In this exercise, make sure your feet are touching.
2. Take a few deep breaths to prepare for the meditation.
3. Hold your hands in front of your body at the chest level, with thumb touching thumb and each finger touching the corresponding finger on the other hand.
4. Close your eyes and take a deep breath. Exhale slowly, and when your lungs are completely empty, hold your breath out for a count of seven.
5. Hold the hand position but relax your breath, taking five or six relaxed, normal breaths. Allow your breath to return to normal.
6. Repeat steps 4 and 5 six more times.
7. Release your hands and breathe normally. Put the whole exercise out of your mind, and let your energy naturally return to balance.

Elemental breathing exercises from the Sufi tradition are used to maintain overall well-being and balance. They activate and balance the five elements within us. Although originating in, or at least making themselves known to the modern world through, the Sufi tradition, I learned these breaths in the elemental practices of witchcraft, so they are compatible with any tradition that recognizes the elements. The colors I learned are a bit different from the traditional Sufi colors, which I list after the exercise, if you'd rather have the traditional version. I've seen several different versions of this exercise over the years, but the basic breathing patterns are always the same.

The Sufi elemental breathing in exercise 17 is a breathing version of Exercise 3: Elemental Connection and Balance. This technique allows you to physically integrate these elemental energies. When you perform these breaths, you have the opportunity to see what elements resonate the easiest and the hardest for you, and where in your body you have potential blocks to your health that can be healed by repeating this exercise regularly. Repeated use of this breathing technique will strengthen your elemental paradigm and fuel your instant magick spells with the power of the elements.

Exercise 17

Elemental Breathing

1. Begin by sitting or standing upright, with a straight spine.

2. Focus on the element of earth and the magnetic field of the planet below. Breathe in and out through your nose, drawing up the magnetic energy of the earth through your feet and legs and through the base of your spine. See the earth energy as a healing green power. Feel the magnetic energy balance with your body, anchoring you. Feel it connect with the earth element in you—your bones and the minerals and trace elements in your body. Feel yourself become purified with the power of the earth, down to your bones. Feel yourself grounded and stable. Perform at least five breaths of the earth element.

3. Focus your attention on the water element. Breathe in through your nose and out through your mouth. Imagine drawing up cool, blue, watery energy from the earth below

and into your belly. Feel it soothe and cool your emotions, and purify your blood. Feel it wipe away all that is impure and unwanted. Feel yourself flexible, fluid, and pure, like water. Perform at least five breaths of the water element.

4. Bring your attention to the fire element. Feel the fire element ignite in the solar plexus, like a red candle flame. Breathe in through your mouth and out through your nose. With each breath, feel the flame grow brighter, illuminating your entire body. Feel the heat of combustion, as your stomach digests your food, your fuel, like the sun burns its own fuel to create light. Throw all that doesn't serve you, particularly anger, into the fire and light, to be purified. Feel the light fill all your cells, energizing them with divine power. Feel the power rise from your solar plexus and illuminate your heart. Feel yourself energized. Perform at least five breaths of the fire element.

5. Bring your attention to the air element. Breathe in and out through your mouth, as the air feeds the light within your heart. Feel the blue air energy move through your entire body as you breathe, cleansing all your organs and tissues of impurities. Feel yourself expand. Feel your creativity grow. Feel yourself release the thoughts that shackle you to an old sense of self. Perform at least five breaths of the air element.

6. Bring your attention to the fifth element, of ether, or akasha, the element of spirit. Breathe in and out through your nose. Feel the energy ascend to the crown and above, like a dazzling rainbow of light flowing in and out of you. Feel your connection to all the elements in you, and feel your connection to all life, everywhere, connected by ether, life force.

7. Gently return your awareness, and breathe normally, feeling the shift of elemental energy within you.

This meditation can be aided by a clock that gives an audible tick, or a metronome, to keep a regular pace for all the breaths. As you develop, you can extend the time you spend on each element as needed, though the ideal is to spend the same amount of time on each. Five breaths per element is usually considered the minimum.

Traditional Sufi colors are yellow for earth, green for water, red for fire, blue for air, and white or rainbow for ether. I use the more traditional Western elemental correspondences for the elements. Some versions of the meditation specify the various colors and energies entering and exiting through specific body parts, but this is the first way I learned this meditation, and it's still my favorite.

Some practitioners use mudras in their elemental breathing. Each of the fingers stands for a specific element and planet (figure 13). When you place your thumb and a particular finger together, you activate that elemental energy within you. Thumb and middle finger together is for the earth element and Saturn. Thumb and index finger is the water element and Jupiter. Thumb and ring finger is the fire element and the Sun. Thumb and pinky finger is the

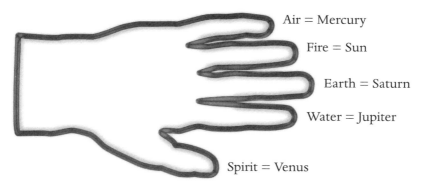

Air = Mercury

Fire = Sun

Earth = Saturn

Water = Jupiter

Spirit = Venus

Figure 13: The Hand and the Elements

air element and Mercury. Try doing the elemental breaths with the corresponding mudra. You do not need to use any mudra for the fifth element.

If you work with a strong elemental paradigm in your instant magick, you can use these mudras instead of your trigger to conjure forth the appropriate energy for your spell. Some Eastern mystics feel that if you touch the thumb with the pad of the finger, the energy is receptive, and appropriate in this meditation. If you put the pad of the thumb to the nail of the finger, the energy is more active and projective, and good for spell work.

Pranic breathing is another form of energized breathing. It's a little less complicated than the previous elemental breaths, though I find it just as powerful, but in a different way. As mentioned in chapter 2, prana is the energy of all things. It is often equated with the fifth element, also known as ether, akasha, or the element of spirit. Prana, a term from India, is also associated with the element of air and the breath, as breathing exercises are known as pranayama. In other parts of the world, the same basic energy is known as chi, ki, mana, or numen. Prana is in the food we eat, in the air we breathe, and all around us and in us. It is the vital life force you felt in Exercise 2: Sensing and Manipulating Energy.

By drawing upon the life force, or prana, from the environment around you, you can increase the healthy flow of energy throughout your body, and direct it wherever it is needed to aid in your healing process.

Exercise 18

Pranic Breathing

1. Focus on the land beneath you. Imagine that your legs, feet, and toes are growing into the roots of a great tree, anchoring and grounding you deeply into the land. Feel yourself connected to the pure heart of the earth. As you inhale, draw up the energy, the prana, of the land. Feel it warm and tingly as it enters your physical body. Program the energy with a heal-

ing intention, such as saying silently, "This energy heals me and balances me in all ways." Do this for a few minutes, until you are comfortable with the intention and sensation.

2. Focus on the sky above. Imagine your crown reaching up to the heavens, growing out like the trunk and branches of a tree, touching the sky. As you inhale, draw down the prana of the sky, the pure energy of the cosmos. You might feel your "branches" connect to the sun, moon, or a particular planet. When in doubt, connect to the energy of the sun, as the purer and more healing prana that is the source of all others in this system. Feel it enter your body via the crown. Program it with the same healing intention you used in step 1. Practice this for a few minutes.

3. On your next inhale, try to draw energy from below and above simultaneously, if you haven't done so already.

4. Imagine the energy of these two worlds meeting in your heart and forming a ball of prana. Imagine that ball like a radiant star, sending out energy to the rest of your body in waves of healing light.

You don't have to formally end this exercise. You can simply let it fade from your consciousness as you turn your attention to other matters. The energy will still flow and heal you for a time. If you need to stop the flow, or you feel overwhelmed by the energy, first imagine stopping the flow from the heavens. Then imagine all the excess prana draining down through your roots into the earth. Make the flow one-way, until all the excess energy is gone. By your will and intention, it will happen.

The last breathing exercise I have to share is pore breathing. There are several different versions of this exercise, in both Eastern and Western traditions. Basically, you look at your skin as part of the energetic respiratory system, allowing it to absorb more prana than you would through normal respiration.

Pore breathing can be a combination of both the traditional elemental breathing and pranic breathing exercises (exercises 17 and 18). Instead of focusing on the chakra column and the duality of above and below, in pore breathing you focus on your entire being, and transfer energy through your skin, and specifically your pores. You focus on a particular intention or quality of energy, and then inhale that intention into every cell in your body, or fill yourself with that quality. Like a sponge, you absorb it through all the tiny holes of your body.

For example, you can breathe in love. Think and feel that emotion strongly around you as you inhale. Feel it being absorbed. Then when you exhale, release whatever you feel is the opposite of love, or whatever prevents you from feeling love more fully. I would imagine either fear or hate. Continue the process until you feel you have filled your body with as much of that energy as you can take.

Pore breathing works with ideals, such as love, joy, peace, or harmony, but can also be used to invest yourself with the qualities of a particular color of energy, such as pink, green, or blue light. Think about the qualities of the color, and the chakras and planets associated with it. You can also use pore breathing to invoke the energy of the elements, either a particular element or all five, like the Sufi breaths. If you want to do a spell that involves a particular element, you can build up a "charge" of that element within you. If you feel you need to bolster a particular element for your healing, you can focus solely on it. Just make sure you don't focus on one element so much that you become out of balance with the others.

Exercise 19

Pore Breathing

1. Sit up straight and supported, in whatever position is comfortable for you. Ideally your back shouldn't be touching a chair, but do whatever you need to do to support your back and be comfortable. Though some say you should have as much skin exposed as possible for this exercise, I've found it works just fine fully clothed.

2. Think of whatever intention you want to breathe in. If there's an opposite to release, think about what you need to release.

3. As you inhale, be very aware of your skin. Feel as if you are breathing in and out through your pores, as if each pore is a little mouth sucking in an energetic breath.

4. Imagine yourself bathed in the energy of your intention. As your pores breathe, they take in the energy of your intention. With each breath it moves deeper, as you exhale the unwanted energies and draw further upon what you want. The energy of your intention becomes a part of you, down to the very bone, circulating throughout your entire body.

5. Feel the energy of your intention build inside you until you have as much as you want and need.

6. When done, you can direct the energy toward either a specific goal, such as healing, or other spell work. You can absorb the energy into your body.

Some practitioners fear that pore breathing is dangerous, that you can overload on energy. Depending on the intention that you breathe in, that's true. If you feel overloaded, simply ground the excess energy into the earth. As with pranic breathing, direct the unwanted energy into the land below, to be grounded and neutralized.

The effect of pore breathing is much like changing the vibration of your energy. One magickal axion, known as the Principle of Vibration, says that all things vibrate, meaning all things—from our bodies, to the elements, to concepts such as love and healing—have a vibration. As you breathe through your pores, you can mentally affirm that you are "vibrating in harmony with" whatever your intention or energy is, making the exercise even more effective.

Techniques for Healing Others

The basic instructions I was given for healing others are simple. First and foremost, make sure you have permission of the recipient of the healing. As already discussed, it is best to obtain conscious permission. If that's not possible, you can ask the recipient's higher self, their divine consciousness, if the healing is for the highest good, when you psychically connect to them. This permission technique is a last resort. Conscious permission is preferred for two reasons. First, it can actively engage the recipient in their own healing path. Second, when we really want to help someone, sometimes our desire to help can cloud our ability to hear the response. Hearing no when we want to help someone can be difficult, so many well-meaning healers will assume the answer is yes, even when the illness or injury is serving the higher good of the intended recipient on some level. The true response can be hard to hear on a personal level, especially when there is suffering involved, but it is necessary on the impersonal soul level.

Once you have the recipient's permission, you can begin the healing. While in a meditative state, mentally picture the recipient in your mind's eye, to the best of your ability. Repeating their name, silently or out loud, particularly if you have never met the recipient, is a great way to connect psychically. Some practitioners will hold a picture of the person, or an object the recipient touched. In magick, when you use an object that another has previously handled to create a magickal connection to that person, you are using the Law of Contagion. This magickal concept states that if two things come into connection, there will always be a connection between them, no matter how far away from each other they are. If the recipient is physically present, you can touch them, but it is not necessary. You are not transferring your personal energy to the person, but gathering the energy of the universe to help heal and transform.

I like to use touch in healing, in this and many other techniques, when possible, but it is also good to make sure you are shielded from picking up any unwanted, unhealthy energy from the ill recipient, so try doing the Psychic Shield spell (chapter 4) before doing healing work. If you receive any impressions that are physically or emotionally uncomfortable for you, acknowledge them and affirm that they will stop. If they do stop, then that was simply how your psyche was relaying information; and once you acknowledge the information, it is no longer necessary. If the uncomfortable impressions don't stop, and you feel you are taking on the illness of the recipient, break contact and try again later. Reaffirm your shields. In the meantime, do your own healing and rebalancing exercises to purify yourself.

Once you have established a connection with the recipient, there are several ways to go about the healing.

Colored Light

Imagine the recipient surrounded by and filled with green light, pure green light gathered from the abundant energy of the universe. You can use the green light for all manner of general healing, to promote immunity, new growth, and vivid health. Envision this color in the shade of newly growing spring plants or the green of a clear emerald. If you need intense healing for a life-threatening situation, use red-orange, like the glowing ember of a flame. Red-orange stimulates the survival mechanism and can heal intensely and quickly, but can be an ordeal in itself. You can use the pore-breathing techniques to help focus and direct the energy as long as you are gathering and directing outside energy, not simply projecting your own. You can also use Exercise 2: Sensing and Manipulating Energy to aid in directing energy. You must build up a "ball" of energy composed of that colored light to direct for the healing. You can transfer this ball of energy through touch if you are physically present with the recipient, or mentally "send" it across the astral plane to the recipient, with the intention that it be for the highest good, harming none. When done, thank and release the recipient. Imagine wiping away their image from your mind as you send them the healing. You are releasing their energy.

Pranic Healing

You can send pure healing energy, pure prana, rather than colored energy, to aid in the healing process. Use pranic breathing to direct energy toward a person in need of healing, via contact if you are physically present with the person. If not, you can will the prana across the astral plane, projecting it from your heart or hands, with the intention that it be for the highest healing good. Then imagine in your mind's eye that the recipient receives the energy and is healed.

Elemental Healing

Just as you can send colored light or pranic energy to someone, you can also send elemental energy. Use Exercise 3: Elemental Connection and Balance, Exercise 17: Elemental Breathing, or the elemental version of Exercise 19: Pore Breathing to connect with the elemental energy. I suggest that you send all five elemental energies, with the intention of health and balance.

When you are done with a healing session, it never hurts to do something to balance yourself, such as an elemental or chakra-balancing exercise, to make sure you haven't taken on any unwanted energies. Make sure to ground yourself after every session, coming back fully into the world and your own energy.

Advanced Color Healing

Later on in my training, with a greater understanding of the energy bodies and the chakras, I learned how a variety of colors can affect health beyond the two colors I initially learned. If you know where the illness or injury is located in the body, determine the color of the chakra closest to it. You can use that color or its complementary color on the color wheel (figure 14) to bring healing. If the area is weak, the color of the chakra will energize it and bolster its power. If the area is overactive, the complementary color can be used to soothe it and calm it down. For example, if a person has an agitated lower digestive system that needs to be soothed and calmed, the natural color of the belly chakra is orange, and its complement is blue, so filling the area with blue light will bring soothing relief. Once the area is calm, a seven-chakra balancing meditation can be done to integrate the healing into the entire system,

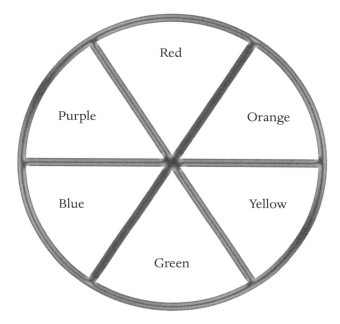

Figure 14: Color Wheel

using the commonly accepted colors of the chakras. You can also use orange light, with the intention of healing the area and bringing it into balance, particularly if the blue light feels unnatural to you because you so strongly associate the belly with orange. Use what works for you.

In the same vein, if you want to heal on the emotional, mental, and spiritual levels and not just the physical, find the chakra that is associated with a particular imbalance, and use that chakra's color, or its comple-ment, to bring a change in your consciousness. True magick alters your consciousness first, so you can respond and adapt to your reality in more balanced and healthy ways. If you are despondent over the end of a romantic relationship and have a broken heart, meditating with the colors of the heart chakra (green and pink) would be appropriate. If your mind is agitated and you can't let go of a thought or image, it might be helpful to meditate with the colors of the throat and third eye chakras (blue and purple) or their respective complements (orange and yellow). At times, you will be drawn to certain colors, in meditation and even in your clothing, without knowing why they call to you; but they are having a subtle balancing effect on your consciousness. Clothing is an excellent way to use color healing when you are having difficulty meditating and concentrating.

Visual Healing Magick

If you have a knowledge of anatomy and biology, you can go beyond the chakras to do some even deeper healing work. Those with a keen interest in the physical sciences and a willingness to apply their knowledge to magick can create some startling results.

Using meditation or your instant magick trigger, you can direct physical healing by visualizing specific actions taking place in the body. If you want to speed up the process of healing a broken bone, imagine the bone cells dividing rapidly and filling in the cracks perfectly. To ease the transition of detoxification, visualize toxins and poisons being flushed from the liver and running harmlessly out of the body. Another tried and true method of healing is to imagine white blood cells sweeping away infections in the body.

A literal knowledge of the body's anatomy and biological processes is exceedingly helpful, but you can also create the same effects through symbolism. You can imagine the bone cells as little workers plastering up the bone like a repair crew. Toxins can pass through water "filters" that are then psychically removed, taking the toxins with them. The white blood cells can be tanks destroying the infections, or animals eating them up. One of my favorite images is the hunting dogs of the Goddess eating up rogue cells that are cancerous. I even used this technique to metabolize unwanted fat when exercising, imagining the fat as lumps of fuel being burned in the furnace of my metabolism. I followed up the vision with the mantra "I am fit, trim, and muscular. I am burning all unwanted fat." I just held my instant trigger while climbing the stair machine. With the proper diet, exercise, supplements, and giving myself time to do it slowly and correctly, I lost fifty pounds.

If you decide to pursue this route of physical healing, I recommend an in-depth study of medical biology and anatomy. Many health institutes have in-depth courses for massage therapists and other nontraditional health professionals. I highly suggest taking the time to gather this knowledge. Learning the medical names is not as important as understanding how and why things work, but using such terminology can make your healing intentions much clearer to your body, and to the universe.

Body Talking

Another great way of working with the body is to use the power of instant magick to connect to your body consciousness, your body wisdom, and ask it what the problem is and how you can help. I call this technique "body talking" because you are both talking to your body and listening to its answer, its needs. The wisdom of your body's elemental consciousness is vast, and it can tell you a lot.

If you have a specific illness or pain, begin by getting into a meditative state. Imagine your mind traveling from your head (even though we know the mind permeates the entire body, as the mental body layer of the aura) to the area of concern, focusing on it. Evoke the spirit of your body. You could say, "I call upon the spirit of my stomach. Please share your knowledge with me. So mote it be." Ask that part of your body what is causing the imbalance and how you can help. Then listen with both your heart and your mind. Follow the intuitions and messages you receive. Your body might give you a specific form of therapy to try, or suggest you see a health care professional. It might ask you to change your diet or change your moods. Listen, and if you are in partnership with your body, take its advice into consideration. Do what your body needs.

Even when you feel completely healthy, try this exercise by scanning your body and giving any parts of your body an opportunity to speak with you and ask for what they need. You can confront potential problems before they ever manifest by having a strong connection to your body, your sacred vehicle in this world.

Minor Psychic Surgery

Rather than flush a system with healing energy to remove blockages, you can directly remove the energy of illness or pain from a person and replace it with healing energy. This is one form of psychic surgery—where one is psychically, not physically, removing illness. Psychic surgery is based on the concept that if you remove the energetic blueprint of the illness, the illness itself will easily collapse and be repaired by the body.

In day-to-day life, you most often see this technique of psychic surgery performed to cure headaches and minor pain. I've watched many aspiring healers attempt to remove the pain of a headache without knowing the basic healing principles, and a short time later they have a headache themselves. They didn't know what to do with the energy, so they absorbed it accidentally.

To remove a harmful energy or pain, imagine extending your fingers, your etheric fingers, several inches longer than your physical fingers. (If you were to place your physical fingertips on someone, your etheric fingertips would extend into the person's body.) I hold the tips of my fingers and imagine that I am stretching them out. If working on someone else, ask them where the pain is and place your fingertips on that area. Imagine your etheric fingertips reaching in and latching on to the pain. Physically pull out the unwanted energy, moving your arms away from the body. Do this several times until there is a significant difference in the harmful energy or pain. You will no longer feel the energy, even if the client is still experiencing pain. Imagine taking the energy in your hand and filling it with a transformative energy, such as violet or white light, or elemental fire energy, transmuting the harmful energy into something clear and benign. You can also physically press the energy into the ground to ground it into the earth, to be transmuted. Make sure you mentally direct it all the way into the earth, particularly if you are on the second floor of a building. You don't want to pollute your downstairs neighbor with unwanted energies. Then perform a healing with colored light or prana over the location where you just removed the energy, filling that space with pure, healing energy, so no harm can return.

More advanced forms of psychic surgery exist, but this technique will start you on the healing path.

Healing with Spirits

The last instant-magick healing technique I want to discuss is healing through the power of your spirit guides. Just as many people believe we have guides to aid us in our lives and guardians to protect us from harm, I believe we have spirits whose job is to physically and spiritually heal us.

The best place to work with our healing spirits is in the inner temple. There is a gateway in the inner temple that leads to our healing spirits and healing energies. I usually meditate in the temple, opening the gateway and letting its healing energy bathe me deeply. The guides "work" on me like a modern-day energy practitioner would. Though I usually sit up to meditate, this is one of the few meditations where I lie down, as if I was on a massage table or healing practitioner table.

Exercise 20

Inner Temple Healing

1. Perform Exercise 11: The Inner Temple to enter your inner temple space. You can do it lying down if you desire.

2. Look around and hold the intention of finding your gateway of healing.

3. Once you find the gateway of healing, but before you open it, ask for the highest and best healing spirit guides to work with you at this time. Hold your intention for healing. What is it that you wish to be healed? It could be a physical illness, psychological issues, or emotional problems in need of healing. Be clear in your intention. If you are not sure, simply ask to be healed in a manner that is for your highest good at this time.

4. Open the gateway. Feel the healing light flowing out of it. The energies will be whatever energies and colors you need at this time. Enter the healing chamber.

5. Feel the healing guides "work" on you. You might feel as if you are on a work table and they are massaging you or performing psychic surgery. Allow them to heal you on all levels. Your best guides and spirits will be present when you open this gateway from the inner temple.

6. You might ask questions about your healing, and receive a response from your guides. Go with your first intuition.

7. When you feel the session is complete, thank your guides for this healing. Return to the main temple, and close the gateway of healing. Once done, return through the world tree tunnel that brought you to this place, and stand before the world tree. Step back through the screen of your mind's eye, and let the world tree gently fade from view. Erase the image of the world tree, and return yourself to normal consciousness. Do any necessary grounding.

As you develop a personal relationship with your guides, they will teach you how to work with them on a deeper level. They will show you more advanced healing skills for yourself and other people, if you choose to work healings for others.

Magickal healing, for yourself and especially for others, is not something to be entered into lightly. Healing carries a great responsibility. These are simple techniques for your personal toolbox to maintain your own health and help others around you. This is not a manual for those seeking to enter the healing arts professionally. That would go beyond the scope of this book. But if you find that you enjoy the healing magick of this book, I encourage you to continue along the path of the healer, and seek out more training in both magickal healing practices and those of our modern alternative healing traditions.

chapter eight

The Magickal Life

As you continue to use magick, it will become ingrained in your life. It will become part of your worldview. You will never look at problems quite the same way, because you will have new skills to help solve them. You will not feel disempowered, because you will know that you are innately connected to the universe, to all things. All things affect you, but you affect all things. There is a reciprocal relationship to everything.

As you delve more deeply into your magickal studies, you will learn about polarities and patterns, and how all things change and shift. Magick workers simply bide their time for the most opportune moments to create change, and patiently listen to the world around them, to know when, and if, change is appropriate.

Slowly you will become the magick. It will become part of every facet of your life. You will become the mystery you seek to solve. At this point, you will hopefully understand the commonality that exists among all people. We are all magick. Some mystics become deluded at this point, feeling they are better than others, more special and more magickal. Their delusions of grandeur only separate them from others and the universe, and defeat the spiritual purposes of magick.

Those who see the commonality of all people realize that we are all magickal beings. We all seek magick. We all do magick. The difference between mystics and nonmystics is that the mystics are conscious of the magick of life. They are actively aware of the magickal forces of the universe interacting with them. They are waiting for others to awaken to the magick. Until then, the others will be doing their own magick, unconsciously and unaware, but magick nonetheless. No one is inherently better than another. Their awareness is just focused on different things. I may be awake to the reality of magick, but slightly sleepy when it comes to calculus. Everybody is valued because of their differences. The math professor applies his own magick, unconsciously and indirectly, to his science, just as the artist, musician, police officer, lawyer, or janitor apply their own brand of magick to their respective disciplines. All aspects of life can be magickal. All acts are rituals and spells. Anything that causes change is magick, and the world is constantly changing.

Thought, Word, and Deed

Every thought you think is magick. Not just you—the witch, mage, or mystic—but everyone. Your thoughts might carry more wattage, be clearer and more focused, and be formed from your will, but basically all your thoughts, magickal and mundane, have the same inherent characteristics as everyone else's. Every thought by every person is energy. It has a vibration. To the magician, thoughts are things. They take shape on the astral plane.

Every word that you say is magick. You might know ancient words of power, secret languages, chants, mantras, and affirmations, but all your words have power, from your everyday words to your scripted spells. What you say and what you write are magick. Your words bring your thoughts into form. Your words give your thoughts a greater vibration, a sonic resonance. Sounds can be used to heal or harm, just like words. Everybody's words have a similar power. Language is symbolic, and speaks not only to the conscious mind but to the body, emotions, and soul. You don't even need to know what a word means to feel the power behind it. When someone praises you in another language, you feel the power of their words. When they curse you in a foreign tongue, this is doubly true.

Your every action is magick. Every movement is an expenditure of energy, directed by your thoughts. Your movements are thoughts put into action. Every action has the potential to create change, from something small to something with greater consequences that we might never know about. In many ways, every act is like a ritual. We tend to be conscious only of the symbolic meanings of magickal and religious rituals, yet every action we take is sacred. It's said that when one reaches a state of enlightenment, each action becomes sacred, because each action is consciously devoted and dedicated to the divine. Each action . . . from every breath, to every bite of food, to every word and deed. From every noble sentiment shared to every bodily function.

When you do something, magickal or mundane, you are creating a change—a change in yourself, in the world around you, and potentially in others, who will react to your actions. Think of how the actions of others, personally, locally, and globally, have affected you. The actions of people with no concept of magick have changed your reality. That's an amazing thought. If magick is truly changing reality in accord with will, there are a lot of mages out there without candles, spell books, and charms. We are all capable of magick.

Collective Reality = Collective Responsibility

We are all creating our shared reality, even those of us who know nothing about magick. We all contribute to the overall vision of the planet and beyond. Our thoughts, words, and deeds affect everyone. This concept is often compared to something called the Butterfly Effect. Scientists speculate that the flapping wings of a butterfly on one continent could be the root cause of a hurricane affecting another continent. We may not see those subtle links to the other side of the world, but they are there. So we have to be careful where and how we flap our wings.

As magickal people, it is imperative that we be even more responsible in our thoughts, words, and deeds because we have claimed more power around them. The more we use our magickal abilities, the more easily and quickly we shape our reality. If we are more aware, we must also be more responsible.

This doesn't mean we should go out and try to convert everyone to a magickal way of living. That's not right for everybody. Many people need to focus their attention in other domains. We can inspire people to perceive magick through our art, music, and writing, but we cannot force our magickal paradigm on anyone. Imagine how you would feel if someone tried to force a different magickal or religious paradigm on you. Everyone must be free to choose where to focus their energy.

What it does mean is that we lead by example. We learn to explore our will, but lead as impeccable a life as possible. It doesn't mean we are perfect, saint-like, or ascended. It means we teach and lead quietly, by example. It was only after I had integrated healthy changes into my own life that I had people ask me to teach them magick. People who saw the transformation in me, who saw how much happier and balanced I was, wanted to know what was different. Only then was I able to share with others how much magick means to me. My definition of magick is very broad, including psychic experiences, spirit work, and most importantly meditation, one of the most powerful magickal tools of all. Magick isn't always about spells, instant magick or otherwise.

Integrating the Magickal Life

These all sound like lofty ideals, but how does one actually live up to them? It's not easy. Learning instant magick will not instantly transform your entire life, but it's a great cornerstone. Keeping in mind that all your thoughts, words, and deeds are forms of magick, think of the essentials of the spell—altered consciousness, intention, and energy. Use them as your guide.

Strong emotion, good or bad, can alter consciousness. Strong will, even when not focused for magick, but focused in anger, can create an intention, even though it might not be completely clear to the conscious mind. Be aware of the energy of every situation. When you are interacting with someone, notice when you react to the person rather than act of your own independent thoughts and feelings. When you feel like someone is energetically pulling your chain or pushing your buttons, you are reacting. It's easy to fall into blind reaction rather than taking a moment to contemplate. We all do it. When you are aware of your consciousness, your will, and the energetics of a situation, you will respond rather than react unconsciously.

Be aware of the magick in every situation and place. Feel the energy. See the sacredness. Find it in nature and in urban settings. Find it at sacred sites and in your own home. Recognize the opportunities you have to choose the best magickal outcomes, for the highest good, through your thoughts, words, and deeds, and take advantage of them.

Be aware of the various energies from your selected magickal paradigms. Feel the influence of the elements, the planets, the web of life and spirits. Be amazed at the perfection of the universe, at how all the systems and connections work so well together.

Study. Learn about the world around you, and its people. Study the history, philosophy, science, and even economics and politics of the world, all of which are inherent in magick. They are all models of a reality. They are all symbol systems for a greater reality, a greater truth. Discern and marvel at the differences in and intricacies of the world.

Most importantly, use your magick! Use your instant magick in everyday life. Use other forms of magick you have learned as you deem necessary. Be thankful for all your magickal workings, for all your successes and all your failures. Acknowledge them and thank divinity, however you see it.

Use your magick every day. It will awaken you to greater depths of spirit. If you continue to do magick with an open heart, you will learn what no instructor or book can really teach you—you will see for yourself that we are all connected. All your actions affect others. This is one of the great mysteries. It can be intellectually learned from a book, but never understood until the mystery is personally revealed to you. If you don't seek out the mystery, you will never become a part of it. Only when you do will you be a part of the magickal transformation of yourself, society, and the world.

appendix

Correspondence Charts

The following are a variety of correspondence charts, presenting information on magickal systems, spirits, energies, and entities one can call upon to craft instant magick. Not every practitioner will gravitate to every type of correspondence. By all means, please keep your magick simple and effective. These are tools of inspiration, to help you find the best way to create your magick. Let your intuition guide you to the best systems. As you may notice, a lot of the corresponding magickal purposes were not covered in the spell chapter of this book. Use them to inspire your own new spells and intentions, based on your needs.

Many of the correspondences are not simple energies, but specific spirits and entities, ranging from angels and elementals to the deities and even to the spirits of animals, plants, and stones. A wise practitioner knows not to call upon entities that he or she knows nothing about. Before you call upon a deity or other entity, do some research. Make sure this is an entity you would like to contact and invite into your life. If you are asking for its aid in your magick, do not be surprised if it asks for your aid in other areas of life. You might want to visit your inner temple and make inner contact with any entities, including even animal, plant and stone spirits, before you ask them to create change in your physical life. Such prior preparation is not only smart magick, but polite. If you are asking for an entity's help, you should establish a relationship with it before you make your request.

Elements

Element	Meanings	Principle	Tools	Colors	Directions	Spirits	Magick
Earth	Physical	Law	Stone, Pentacle	Green, Brown, Black	North	Uriel, Ghob	Healing, Home, Prosperity, Strength, Stability, Fertility, Protection, Crystalization
Water	Emotional/ Astral	Love	Cup, Cauldron	Blue, Green, Silver, Purple	West	Gabriel, Niksa	Relationship, Family, Love, Happiness, Cleansing, Healing, Rebirth
Air	Mental	Life	Sword, Blade	Yellow, Sky Blue	South, East	Raphael, Paralda	Communication, Clarity, Memory, Expression, Truth
Fire	Spiritual/ Will	Light	Wand, Torch	Red, Orange, Yellow	East, South	Michael, Djinn	Creation, Spirituality, Passion, Drive, Vitality, Purification, Energy

Three Worlds of Shamanic Cosmology

World	Self	Consciousness	Entities	Magick
Upper World	Higher Self	Superconsciousness	Sky Deities, Angelic Spirits, Ascended Masters	Enlightenment, Spirituality, Knowledge, Information
Middle World	Middle Self	Personality/Ego, Body	Elementals, Nature Spirits	Change, Cycles, Seasons, Healing, Balance, Fertility, Prosperity
Lower World	Lower Self	Unconscious, Intuition	Chthonic Spirits, Ancestors	Healing, Facing Fear, Rejuvenation, Cleansing, Relationship, Revealing Hidden Things, Mysteries of Death

Triplicity

Principle	Astrology	Greek Fates	Norse Fates	Hindu Deities	IAO Formula	Magick
Generation	Cardinal	Clotho	Urd	Brahma	Isis	Creation, Initiation, Beginnings, Evoking
Organization	Fixed	Lachesis	Verdandi	Vishnu	Osiris	Preserving, Sustaining, Supporting
Dissolving/Destructive	Mutable	Atropos	Skuld	Shiva	Apophis	Changing, Removing, Starting Over, Banishing

Chakras

Location	Subtle Body	Colors	Principles	Magick
Root	Physical	Red	Survival, Pleasure	Sexuality, Prosperity, Protection
Belly	Etheric	Orange	Intimacy, Trust, Creativity	Sexuality, Relationships, Intuition, Instincts
Solar Plexus	Astral	Yellow	Power, Self-Image, Energy	Overcoming Fear, Healing, Vitality, Enthusiasm
Heart	Emotional	Green	Emotion	Family, Relationships, Friendships, Society
Throat	Mental	Blue	Communication	Creative Expression, Speaking Up, Listening
Third Eye	Psychic	Purple/Indigo	Vision	Increasing Psychic Power, Visions, Magick
Crown	Divine	White/Violet	Divinity	Connecting to the Higher Self, Seeing the Higher Purpose

Planets

Planet	Colors	Day	Zodiac Signs	Principles	Magick
Sun	Gold, Yellow	Sunday	Leo	Energy, Life	Health, Vitality, Success, Creativity, Prosperity
Moon	Silver, Purple	Monday	Cancer	Emotion, Intuition	Psychic Ability, Tides, Divination, Emotional Healing, Feminine Mysteries
Mercury	Orange	Wednesday	Gemini, Virgo	Mind	Communication, Memory, Logic, Language, Ideas, Travel, Magick
Venus	Green	Friday	Taurus, Libra	Attraction	Personal Love, Romance, Relationships, Art, Music, Pleasure, Sensuality, Money, Things Valued
Mars	Red	Tuesday	Aries	Will	Force, Initiation, Protection, Power, Passion, Anger, Direct Action, Drive, Warrior Skills, Sexual Drive
Jupiter	Blue, Purple	Thursday	Sagittarius	Expansion	Higher Self, Wisdom, Grace, Good Luck, Prosperity, Purpose, Teaching, Learning, Peace, Tranquility

Saturn	Black	Saturday	Capricorn	Contraction	Protection, Binding, Karma, Time, Density, Gravity, Pressure
Uranus	Electric Blue		Aquarius	Innovation	Rebellion, Breaking Limits, Individuality, Freedom, Unorthodoxy, Higher Ideals, Technology
Neptune	Sea Green		Pisces	Unconditional Love	Creativity, Inspiration, Dreams, Romance, Art, Music, Dance
Pluto	Scarlet, Black		Scorpio	Transformation	Destruction, Death, Rebirth, Underworld, True Will, Power, Energy, Awareness, Sexuality, Obsession

Magickal Colors

Color	Elements	Chakra	Planets	Magick
Red	Fire, Earth	Root	Mars	Energy, Vitality, Protection, Grounding, Warrior, Strength
Orange	Fire, Air, Water	Belly	Mercury, Moon	Communication, Intuition, Expression, Sexuality, Feeling
Yellow	Fire, Air	Solar Plexus	Sun	Power, Vitality, Energy, Strength, Fear, Ego, Self-Esteem, Inspiration, Healing, Enlightenment
Green	Earth, Water, Air	Heart	Venus, Neptune	Love, Relationships, Emotion, Attraction, Money, Creativity, Growth, New Life, Health
Blue	Water, Air	Throat	Jupiter, Mercury	Peace, Prosperity, Communication, Understanding, Expression
Purple	Water, Air	Third Eye	Jupiter, Moon	Spirituality, Intuition, Psychic Ability, Expansion
Violet	Water, Fire	Crown	Jupiter, Moon	Transmutation, Awareness, Magick
White	All	Crown	Uranus, Pluto	All-Purpose, Purity, Insight, Light, Union, Harmony

Black	Earth	Root	Saturn, Pluto	Protection, Grounding, Invisibility, Karma, Binding
Brown	Earth	Root	Earth, Saturn	Grounding, Animal Healing, Nature Spirits
Pink	Water	Heart	Venus	Self-Love, Self-Esteem, Unconditional Love
Gold	Fire	Solar Plexus, Heart	Sun, Venus	Light, Inspiration, Intelligence, Divine Masculine, Purity
Silver	Water	Belly	Moon	Intuition, Psychic Ability, Healing, Divine Feminine

170 | Appendix

Elemental Spirits

Name	Type	Magick
Djinn	Ruler of Fire Elementals	Creation, Passion, Identity, Will, Energy, Purification
Ghob	Ruler of Earth Elementals	Prosperity, Health, Home, Finance, Stability, Protection
Niksa	Ruler of Water Elementals	Relationships, Love, Family, Healing, Cleansing, Rebirth
Paralda	Ruler of Air Elementals	Communication, Clarity, Memory, Truth, Expression
Salamanders	Fire Elementals	Classically, fire elementals manifest as red lizards and can aid all manner of fire magick. They help you find your true will and fulfill your desires.
Gnomes	Earth Elementals	Classically, earth elementals manifest as small men and can aid all earth magick, from prosperity to gardening.
Undines	Water Elementals	Classically, water elementals appear as mer-folk, like the popular mermaid image. They can aid in all water magick, particularly love.
Sylphs	Air Elementals	Classically, air elementals appear as small faery-like beings—small and thin, with gossamer wings. They are used in all air magick, including memorization and communication.
Michael	Archangel of Fire	Michael is known as the keeper of the flaming sword or spear. He is also known for his gifts of protection and healing, particularly cutting ties with those who are no longer healthy for us.

Uriel	Archangel of Earth	Uriel is known as the keeper of the pentacle. He gives food, shelter, and physical healing.
Gabriel	Archangel of Water	Gabriel is the messenger, the keeper of the trumpet. As the archangel of water, he delivers messages of the heart. Gabriel is also the keeper of the holy grail of immortality, healing, and unconditional love.
Raphael	Archangel of Air	Raphael is known as the divine physician, bringing the body into balance. He carries the healing wand and is known to bring clarity and peace.

Various shamanic traditions place animal spirits as the guardians of the four directions and elements, rather than archangels or elemental beings. In purpose, they serve similar functions, but manifest in the form of power animals.

Archangels & Angels

Angel	Magick
Asariel	This angel is associated with Neptune and can be called upon for meditation, mediumship, trancework, creativity, dreams, and healing addictions.
Cassiel	This angel is associated with Saturn and can be called upon for protection, when working out karma, and to overcome any obstacle.
Gabriel	Gabriel is the archangel of the Moon and the element of water. He can be called upon for healing, dreams, psychic ability, and emotional clarity. Gabriel helps connect us to our higher self, being the messenger of the higher self through our psychic abilities and intuitions.
Haniel	Haniel is the archangel of Venus and is associated with the nature realm, plant spirits, and faeries. He can be called upon in love magick and to heal relationships.
Michael	Michael is the archangel of fire and the Sun, though some say Mercury. He can assist in magick involving legal matters, achievements, rulership and authority, protection, and health and well-being.
Raphael	Raphael is the archangel of air and Mercury, though some say the Sun. He can assist in all matters of communication, contracts, written creative works, and healing on all levels.
Raziel	Raziel is the archangel of hidden knowledge and is sometimes associated with Neptune.

Sachiel	This angel is associated with Jupiter and can be called upon in magick regarding finances, money, business, legal disputes, and good fortune.
Samael	Samael is the archangel of Mars and can be used in all magick regarding warriors, courage, perseverance, protection, and physical prowess. Samael helps us overcome difficult challenges. Some systems regard Samael as a less-than-pure figure.
Sandalphon	Sandalphon is the archangel of the earth and the material world. He can be called upon to balance the four elements, to manifest your will into reality, and to guide you in the world.
Tzadkiel	This archangel is associated with Jupiter and Mercury as well as magick, transmutation, and wisdom.
Tzafkiel	Tzafkiel is the archangel of Saturn and a protector against spiritual strife and discord.
Uriel	Uriel is the archangel of earth, but is also associated with Uranus. Uriel leads us in the world and is sometimes associated with the angels of death, interring our body back to the earth upon death. Uriel is associated with power in general, and electricity in particular, and is a patron of all electronic equipment.

Deities

Though this is not a comprehensive list of deities by any means, you can use it as a springboard for your own research. I've tended to include deities from pantheons that I've had more personal experience with, focusing on those that appear the most in the Western magick and modern pagan traditions, along with a few favorites from the East. You might find your instant magick allies in the pantheons of other cultures not listed here. Some might find it disrespectful to call upon deities for instant magick, but I personally feel the divine is involved in everything from our most lofty magick to our most mundane hopes and needs.

I believe it's prudent to build a relationship with deities before you go calling on them to help you in daily life. You can start by reading about the history and myths of the deity, to help you make both an intellectual and spiritual connection. Then meditate with the deity, using your inner temple meditation as a launch pad to experience this deity directly. Everybody has a different experience with these godforms when working with them directly. Our modern experiences become the basis of modern magick and legend, though we are respectful of the past. Even when researching past information, we can find conflicting information from different time periods, cultures, and traditions, all on the same deity. That is when you must trust your direct experience with the divinity. Once you have made contact, you can then call upon the deity for aid in daily life. If you take the time to do the necessary background work, you will find that your magick is much more powerful and more harmonious with your spiritual life.

Deities

Name	*Magick*
Agni	Hindu god of fire, earth, sky, and storms. He is the slayer of demons and mediator between humanity and the gods.
Amaterasu	Japanese goddess of the sun.
Amon-Ra	Egyptian aspect of the sun god Ra. Known as the ruler, the divine pharaoh king.
Anubis	Jackal-headed god of Egypt. Patron guide to souls. Inventor of the embalming process. Called upon in healing and medicine.
Aphrodite	Greek goddess of love. She is called upon for spells of attraction, romance, beauty, fertility, and nature. She was born of the foamy ocean, and when she walked upon the land, wildflowers grew in her steps, giving her associations with both the sea and land. She is known as Venus to the Romans.
Apollo	Greek god of the sun, and a patron of poetry, music, sports, healing, and prophecy.
Artemis	Warrior huntress and virgin maiden of the Greek pantheon. Associated with the silver crescent of the moon. Protector of women, children, and animals. Known as Diana to the Romans.
Asclepius	Greek god associated with medicine and healing.
Astarte/ Ishtar	Middle Eastern goddess associated with the planet Venus, as well as love, fertility, the heavens, and the earth.

Deities (cont.)

Name	*Magick*
Athena	Greek goddess of wisdom, ingenuity, weaving, warriors, and battle strategy. She is known to outthink her enemies before fighting them. Known as Minerva to the Romans.
Bel	Celtic god associated with the waxing sun. A god of light, fire, and sexuality. His feast day is Beltane.
Brid	Celtic goddess also known as Bridget and later associated with St. Bridget. She is known as a triple goddess of fire and light as well as healing springs, with an aspect devoted to healing, poetry, and smithcraft.
Ceridwen	Celtic goddess associated with the cauldron of inspiration and rebirth. She is a patron to bards and a teacher of shamanic shapeshifting.
Cernunnos	Celtic horned god, known as the Lord of Animals and Master of the Wild Hunt. He is the guardian of the gateway between the worlds and a protective father figure to many.
Chandra	Hindu moon god associated with the intoxicating beverage of the gods. God of the inner planes, dreams, and psychic ability.
Chronos	Greek god of time, fertility, harvest, and the golden age. Eventually deposed by his children, the Olympians, lead by Zeus. Known as Saturn to the Romans.
Dagda	Celtic all father, known for his cauldron of abundance. Patron of magick, music, and wisdom.
Danu	Celtic mother goddess, associated with the land, sea, and harvest. Mother of the gods.

Demeter   Greek goddess of the grain and all growing things. Associated with motherhood. She and her daughter Persephone are responsible for the changing seasons. Known as Ceres to the Romans.

Durga   Hindu war goddess and protector.

Ea   Sumerian god of land and water, but known as the patron of arts, crafts, civilization, technology, and magickal knowledge.

Enlil   Sumerian god of the land and adviser to the other gods. Known for his wisdom.

Freyja   Norse goddess of magick, fertility, nature, love, and sex. Great goddess in the Norse Vanir pantheon.

Freyr   Norse god of fertility and nature. Brother to Freyja.

Gaia   Greek earth mother. Called upon for all fertility magick. Known for the gifts of prophecy to the priestess at the Temple of Delphi. Tellus Mater is her Roman name.

Ganesha   Hindu god with the head of an elephant. He is known as the remover of all obstacles and the granter of luck and wisdom.

Goibnui   Celtic smith god also associated with jewelry and brewing.

Gwydion   Celtic god of science, light, illusions, magick, and shapeshifting.

Hades   Greek god of the underworld, death, and buried riches. He is called upon in rituals of transformation and rebirth along with other deities of the underworld. Known as Pluto to the Romans.

Deities (cont.)

Name	Magick
Haephastus	Greek forge god married to Aphrodite. Known for his weapons and inventions. Known as Vulcan to the Romans.
Hathor	Egyptian cow goddess, known as a nurturing, healing goddess. Associated with Sekhmet and Bast at various times in Egyptian history and in various magickal traditions.
Hecate	Greek triple goddess of the underworld and crossroads as well as the sky, sea, and land. Crone goddess associated with death, witchcraft, and transformation. The Romans know her as Trivia.
Hel	Norse goddess of the dead and the underworld. The top of her body is a beautiful woman, while from the waist down she is a decaying corpse.
Helios	Greek titan of the sun.
Hermes	Greek god of messengers, gamblers, and magicians. Hermetic magick is named after him as Hermes Trismegistus, or triple great Hermes. Known for his trickster cleverness, his inventions, and his ability to speak well in difficult situations.
Horus	This Egyptian falcon-headed god is the son of Isis and Osiris. He is both the divine child of Isis and the avenger of his father's murder at the hands of his uncle Set. He is connected with the sun, justice, vengeance and the new age.
Imhotep	Egyptian god of healing. A human who was deified.

Indra   Hindu deity of storms, thunder, lightning, war, and fertility.

Isis   The Egyptian mother figure. Isis is known as a master magician, knowing the secret name of the creator god Ra, giving her power over life and death. She resurrected her husband, Osiris, from the dead and aided her son, Horus, in his quest for the throne.

Kali   The dark goddess of the Hindu tradition, Kali is known as both mother nature and mother death. She is a powerful goddess of transformation, facing fear, and surrendering the ego.

Khnemu   Ram-headed Egyptian god who is patron to potters, molders, and sculptors. He is credited with fashioning humankind out of clay on his wheel.

Loki   The Norse trickster god, associated with mischief, lies, and shapechanging. Also associated with light and fire. Many would suggest that Loki is not an appropriate deity for instant magick, as the results will not always be what you wanted or in your best interest, unless you have a close and healthy relationship with the god.

Lugh   Irish Celtic god associated with the harvest festival. He has many skills and his magick can be called upon for many tasks, but in particular he is known in the modern era as a sun and grain god, with skills of the warrior, poet, magician, gamesman, and healer.

Deities (cont.)

Name	Magick
Macha	Celtic goddess of crows and horses. One of the goddesses that make up the Morrighan. I have called upon Macha for protection, both physical and psychic, and for assistance in magick, communication, learning, and speaking.
Marduk	Sumerian king of the gods. Marduk slew the goddess monster Tiamat to create the world. Known as a god of divine justice and keeper of the great cycles.
Merlin	Celtic wizard figure of the British Isles best known for his role in the Arthurian myths.
Morpheus	Greek god of dreams. His father is Hypnos, the god of sleep, and his brothers are Phoebetor and Phantasus, who are also associated with dreams, but with dream warnings and punishments, respectively.
Morrighan	Celtic war goddess who is triple in nature. Goddess of the land, underworld, war, sexuality, victory, and death.
Nabu	Sumerian scribe god.
Nuit	Egyptian star and sky goddess.
Odin	Norse all-father deity. He is both a mercurial wanderer and magician, who used divine sacrifice for wisdom and to gain the runes, as well as a leader of the gods. His magick is for inspiration, warriors, kings, and madmen.

Ogma — Celtic god and warrior associated with poetry, eloquence, and the ogham script alphabet.

Osiris — Egyptian god of the underworld. Originally a god of life and fertility, he was killed by his brother Set and resurrected by his sister-wife, Isis. His magick is for civilization, resurrection, life, death, and immortality.

Pan — Greek god of nature. Horned god with goat legs and horns. Patron of woodlands, animals, passion, sexuality, music, fear, and panic.

Persephone — Greek goddess of the underworld and wife of Hades. She is the goddess of both life and death, ruling the cycles of the seasons with her rise and fall from the underworld. Formerly known as the maiden Kore and known to the Romans as Proserpina.

Poseidon — Greek god of the oceans and storms. He is known to grant safe passage to travelers by sea. Later fused with the Roman water god Neptune.

Prometheus — Greek titan figure who rebelled against the gods to bring fire to humankind. Known as both a rebel and an innovator.

Ptah — Egyptian god of craftsmen. Known as a creator of the universe in some myths.

Quan Yin — Asian goddess of mercy, compassion, and healing. Patron of women and children.

Deities (cont.)

Name	Magick
Ra	Egyptian sun god whom some sources credit as the creator of the universe. He is the god of power, creation, life, and death.
Sarasvati	Hindu goddess of poetry, science, music, creativity, and education.
Seb/Geb	Egyptian earth god.
Sekhmet	Egyptian lion-headed goddess, associated with both the destructive aspects of the sun and its ability to destroy illness.
Selene	Greek goddess of the moon. Associated with dreams, fertility, and magick. Known as Luna to the Romans.
Seshat	Egyptian goddess and consort of Thoth. Goddess of books, libraries, writing, archives, calculations, time, history, stars, and inventions.
Shamash	Sumerian solar deity.
Shiva	Hindu deity known as the dissolver of form. Part of the trinity with Brahma and Vishnu. One of the primal powers of the Hindu pantheon.
Thor	Norse god of thunder, lightning, and storms. God of protection for villagers and common people, as his father, Odin, is the patron of kings, magicians, and berserkers. Associated with Jupiter and good fortune.

Thoth   Egyptian scribe and magician god. Deity of teaching, magic, writing, and civilization. Adviser to the gods, though some sources cite him as creator of the universe.

Uranus   Greek sky father and first consort of Gaia.

Vishvakarma   Hindu god of smiths, architects, builders, weapons makers, and craftsmen.

Weiland   Germanic smith and forge god. He is also associated with the faery realm, horses, and shapeshifting.

Zeus   Greek father god and ruler of the Olympians. Deity of the sky, storms, and lightning. Giver of divine law and justice. Also a very sexual god. Known as Jupiter to the Romans.

Ascended Masters

The ascended masters represent a group of human beings said to have "ascended" from physical consciousness and incarnations to a more exalted state beyond the wheel of life, death, and rebirth. There they remain, postponing union with the divine to aid all of humanity in achieving this same state of union with the divine. Though there are many masters from many spiritual cultures and traditions, here I have focused on the masters, or cohens, of the seven rays. The seven-ray system is a way to categorize psychology, spirituality, and esoterics, based in modern Theosophy and best known through the many works of Alice Bailey. Unlike other aspects of magick, the qualities of the ascended masters are often more spiritually concerned and abstract compared to the more concrete issues found in pagan magick systems.

El Moyra	Master of the first (red) ray, warriors, leadership, courage
Hilarion	Master of the fifth (orange) ray, science, technology, new thoughts, psychic prediction
Kuthumi	Master of the second (blue) ray, philosophy, math, geometry, music, devotional love
Paul the Venetian	Master of the fourth (green) ray, art, creativity, nature (some channelers state that Paul is the master of the third ray)
Sananda	Master of the sixth (indigo) ray, religion, devotion, prayer, monastic life
Serapis Bey	Master of the third (yellow) ray, higher mind, abstract thought, intellectualism, tolerance, discipline (some channelers state that Serapis Bey is the master of the fourth ray)
St. Germain	Master of the seventh (violet) ray, ceremonial magick, transmutation, healing, mystery societies

Animal Spirits

When you use animal spirits for instant magick, you are calling upon the overarching spirit of a particular kind of animal, what some might call the archetypal being, to grant its mystical power to you. As each animal contains a particular brand of mystical teachings and insights, referred to as that animal's medicine, you are asking it to grant you its medicine to fulfill a specific purpose in your life. You should undertake a thorough study of animal wisdom in the shamanic paradigm if you are drawn to doing instant magick with the aid of animal spirits. My book *The Temple of Shamanic Witchcraft* has extensive information on animal spirit medicine, and how to partner with your animal spirit for healing and guidance.

Animal Spirits

Animal	Magick
Ant	Helps with magick to get organized, to form group consciousness or community spirit. Sacred to the goddesses of the underworld.
Badger	Badger spirit is a patron to healers, for those who have to dig out the root of a problem and heal completely.
Bat	Use the magick of Bat if you want to create fear. Bat is called upon to create change through confronting the problem. Bat magick is also for navigating without the use of sight.
Bear	Bear medicine is power and strength, yet also calm introspection.
Beetle	Used in any form of transformation magick. In Egyptian lore, the beetle god pushes the sun up from the underworld.
Blue Jay	Call on Blue Jay spirit in spells of communication when you fear you are not being heard or not being assertive.
Buffalo	The sacred magick of Buffalo is prosperity and abundance, but also the creativity in using everything to its fullest capacity.
Bull	Used in magick requiring virility and stamina.
Butterfly	Butterfly magick is for expressing your unique and creative self to help you transform.

Cat   Call upon Cat to aid in psychic ability, intuition, instincts, and shamanic journey. Used to connect with the lunar energies of the moon.

Coyote   Coyote magick is used when tricks need to be played. Also used for evoking a sense of humor and the ability to laugh at ourselves.

Cow   The magick of Cow is the magick of nourishment, prosperity, and unconditional love.

Crab   The magick of Crab is for protection and security, particularly around the family, or protecting your home.

Crow   Crow is another trickster magician like Coyote. Crow is used for shamanic journey magick, protection, transformation divination, and spells of communication.

Deer   Deer magick is used when the qualities of gentle love and compassion are needed.

Dog   Use this magick for protection, companionship, and unconditional love.

Dolphin   Dolphin magick is for all spells requiring us to get into rhythm or to balance our breath. Also used in any dream magick and in general with the element of water.

Dragonfly Used to break illusions, to see reality as it truly is.

Eagle   Eagle magick is to connect with the divine for guidance and understanding. Eagle helps us receive messages from the gods and spirits. Eagle is also a regal bird connected with the sky king gods, conveying power and wisdom.

Animal Spirits (cont.)

Animal	Magick
Fox	Fox magick is for invisibility, camouflage, and cunning.
Frog	Call on this animal spirit to purify, to tune in to your environment, and to find your voice.
Goat	Work with the spirit of Goat to climb higher and to go beyond your self-imposed limitations. Goat magick is used for prosperity, success, and having the will to get where you want to be.
Goose	Goose is also called upon to find your voice, and to receive early warnings of danger.
Horse	Horse adds power to all magick, and is particularly potent in travel and travel protection spells.
Lion	The magick of Lion is for leadership, success, and prosperity.
Lizard	Use Lizard magick for dream spells and for any act of regeneration and healing.
Mosquito	Mosquito medicine is used to remove fear. Mosquito is also a teacher of patience.
Mouse	The magick of Mouse is used to increase the sensitivity of the senses other than sight.
Otter	Otter spirit is called on in spells dealing with motherhood, children, play, and feminine energy.
Owl	Owl magick is for divination, astral travel, true sight, and wisdom.
Porcupine	Porcupine magick is for protection and defense.
Rabbit	Work with the spirit of Rabbit for creativity, fertility, and facing your fears.
Ram	Call on Ram for leadership skills, courage, and facing fears.

Raven	Raven is used for all manner of magick, being a spirit that is connected with the powers of creation. Raven is particularly good for communication, artistic inspiration, transformation, and navigating in the dark.
Rooster	Use Rooster magick to wake up in the morning and for male virility and protection of the sacred feminine.
Salmon	In Celtic lore, Salmon is known for the power of poetic inspiration and memory, as a sacred totem to the bards.
Sea Horse	Spells calling upon Sea Horse are for love and fidelity, as well as understanding gender roles and role reversal.
Snake	Snake is the power of regeneration through shedding your old skin. It also helps with grounding. The python, as part of the worship of Mother Gaia, is known for its powers of prophecy in the Temple of Delphi.
Spider	Spider magick grants the powers of creativity, writing, self-expression, patience, and detachment.
Squirrel	Use Squirrel spirit to prepare for the future, to plan, gather, and store. Squirrel spirit can be used in financial planning and investment magick.
Swan	Swan works with beauty magick, both inner and outer beauty. Swan also gives the ability to be graceful and coordinated in all manner of movement and dance.
Turtle	Turtle's main power is its shell, the power of protection. It is also called upon for grounding, centering, and connecting with the Earth Mother goddess.

Animal Spirits (cont.)

Animal	Magick
Whale	Whale magick aids in the memorization and retelling of stories, records, and history. Whale also helps with spells involving the voice or singing.
Wolf	Wolf is another strong totem called for protection, particularly protection of the family. In Native lore, the wolf is known as the teacher, and is the patron to all teachers, but in particular spiritual teachers.

Plant Spirits

When using plant spirits as patrons in your instant magick, you do not literally need to have the plant present. You don't have to harvest, cut, or carry it with you. You do not ingest it as a tea or tincture. You call upon the presence of the plant's spirit, the guiding force that develops its physical, magickal, and spiritual qualities. Sometimes evoking and working with a plant spirit is as effective as working with an herbal extract physically. Some traditions teach that everybody has a power plant spirit. As with animal spirits, it helps to develop a relationship with the plant spirits. You can develop a relationship through growing, harvesting, and using the herbs in your life, with the guidance of a good medicinal and magickal herbal book; but once you make a connection to a plant spirit and it becomes your ally, you can call upon it for aid in your instant magick, without having any of the physical herbs present with you.

Plant Spirits

Name	Magick
Aconite	Aconite plant spirit is used to aid astral travel and for introspection, guidance, and protection. Do not use the physical herb, as it is poisonous.
Angelica	Use Angelica to connect with spirit guides, angels, and ancestors. It confers protection from the upper world.
Basil	Basil is used in love and sex magick, as well as purification and protection.
Blackberry	An herb of protection used to connect with the dark goddess energies. Used to remove illness and unwanted forces.
Bleeding Heart	Use its magick for healing your heart from hurtful relationships or situations.
Catnip	Call on Catnip to connect with your instincts and psychic abilities.
Chamomile	Used for sleep, dream, and relaxation magick.
Chickweed	When Chickweed is called on, its energy brings a cooling and soothing quality to any situation.
Cinquefoil	Cinquefoil is used in protection magick as well as astral travel.
Comfrey	Whenever you want to build something, the energy of Comfrey creates structure and stability. Also used in past-life exploration.
Daffodil	Called upon for communication, with both people and spirits.

Dandelion	Dandelion has many uses, including healing, grounding, prosperity, and cleansing.
Juniper	The spirit of Juniper grants prosperity and fulfills dreams.
Lavender	This spirit brings peace, upliftment, prosperity, and protection.
Mandrake	As a spirit medicine, Mandrake aids in shamanic journey, protection, power, love, lust, and fertility. Do not use the physical herb, as it is poisonous.
Money Plant	Used for prosperity. Also used to connect to the moon, for its Latin name is Lunaria.
Morning Glory	Used to awaken energies that lie dormant within you.
Mugwort	Aids in shamanic journey, psychic ability, purification, and protection.
Peppermint	Peppermint spirit aids in mental stimulation, clarity, and communication, and helps the memory.
Rose	The power of Rose is the power to open the heart and to love. Also used for protection.
St. John's Wort	Use this powerful plant spirit to protect, to uplift the spirit, and as an aid in dream magick.
Valerian	Used in dream magick and to aid in sleep.
Vervain	All-purpose herb, used for protection, love, purification, and psychic ability.
Vinca	The Vinca flower, also known as the Sorcerer's Violet, opens the third eye and psychic ability, while conferring protection.
Water Lily	Opens the crown chakra to higher spiritual forces and the guidance of higher beings.
Yarrow	Classically, Yarrow is used for love magick, but also for protection shields, to help us set boundaries.

Stone Spirits

As with plant spirits, you do not need the physical substance present when calling upon stone spirits in your instant magick. You are calling upon the spirit of the stone, the living energy that guides its physical, magickal, and spiritual properties. Like plants and animals, minerals have a spiritual consciousness, and can be called upon to aid your magick. Crystal magicians and healers find that once they have a strong relationship with a stone, they don't need to have it physically present to channel its power. You too can call upon the stone spirits to aid in your instant magick. I do suggest that you build a relationship with the stones before you call upon them. Obtain a small piece of stone and carry it with you for a time. Meditate on it. Really get to know its color, its vibration, and its personality. Different stones have different personalities, just like plants, animals, and people. Each stone resonates with different parts of life. Then, once you have a connection, you can confidently call upon the spirit of the stone when doing your magick, without having your small stone piece with you.

Stone Spirits

Stone	Magick
Amethyst	Amethyst brings peace, tranquility, and clarity. Its energy is for expansion and inspiration, and can be used to fuel artistic endeavors or for traditional prosperity magick.
Bloodstone	Bloodstone spirit is energizing, giving a warrior-like strength and courage.
Carnelian	Carnelian boosts creativity and intuition. It can also be used in magick that requires endurance.
Citrine	Citrine increases the power of light and can be used for healing, inspiration, insight, prosperity, and power.
Emerald	Emerald is used for love, prosperity, physical healing, and to be able to see the world clearly.
Fluorite	Fluorite is a stone of protection, strengthening the auric boundary, cleansing, and absorbing unwanted pain. Blue, Green and Purple Fluorite can be used for prosperity, while Pink Fluorite is used for love. Clear Fluorite is an all-purpose protection stone and can be used to create a sense of personal space.
Garnet	Garnet generates heat and can be used in all fire magick, but also has a strong earth connection and is used in grounding and protection.
Jasper	Jasper is an all-purpose stone, used for healing, protection, strength, endurance, and past-life memories.
Kyanite	Kyanite directs energy on the mental plane, and can be used for communication, clarity, and creativity. It also removes unhealthy thoughts and mental blocks.

Stone Spirits (cont.)

Stone	Magick
Lapis Lazuli	Lapis Lazuli is used in manifesting prosperity—both physical riches and spiritual riches. It promotes creativity, lifts depression, and can be used in any form of communication magick.
Malachite	Malachite energy is strongly associated with the earth, and is used for grounding, prosperity, physical healing, and absorbing pain.
Moonstone	Moonstone magick connects you to the moon and to the moon goddess, and can be used in balancing all forms of inner and outer cycles, particularly emotional balance and feminine menstruation cycles. Moonstone opens the gates of intuition and psychic ability, and gives us more conscious access to the dream world.
Moss Agate	Connects to the nature realms of plants and plant spirits.
Obsidian	Obsidian is used to fulfill all manner of wishes and in divination and introspection work. Just be careful what you wish for. Reflecting on your desire before setting it into motion with your instant magick is a healthy thing to do with Obsidian magick.
Onyx	Onyx has many qualities associated with healing grief, but the stone's energy is most notable for its ability to block and ground harmful energy. Some find its energy too blocking and feel psychically blocked when wearing a lot of onyx, so if you call upon this stone spirit often, be aware of this side effect.

Quartz	Clear Quartz energy is an all-purpose amplifier. Call upon it to amplify your instant magick intention whenever you feel you need to bolster your will.
Rose Quartz	Use Rose Quartz energy to heal the emotional body, strengthen self-esteem, and promote creativity.
Ruby	Ruby is a fire stone, amplifying the power set into motion with your magick. Ruby stimulates the immune system, and can be used to accomplish any goal you really desire.
Turquoise	Turquoise is another all-purpose stone, best known for healing, peace, protection, tranquility, and communication.

Bibliography

Andrews, Ted. *Animal-Speak: The Spiritual & Magical Powers of Creatures Great & Small.* St. Paul, MN: Llewellyn Publications, 1993.

Beyerl, Paul. *A Compendium of Herbal Magick.* Custer, WA: Phoenix Publishing, 1998.

———. *The Master Book of Herbalism.* Custer, WA: Phoenix Publishing, 1984.

Bonewits, Isaac. *Real Magic.* York Beach, ME: Samuel Weiser, 1989.

Bruyere, Rosalyn L. *Wheels of Light.* New York: Fireside Publishing, 1989.

Cabot, Laurie. *Witchcraft as a Science, I and II.* Class handouts and lecture notes. Salem, MA: 1993.

Cabot, Laurie, with Jean Mills. *Celebrate the Earth: A Year of Holidays in the Pagan Tradition.* New York: Dell Publishing, 1994.

Cabot, Laurie, and Tom Cowan. *Love Magic: The Way to Love Through Rituals, Spells and the Magical Life.* New York: Dell Publishing, 1992.

Cabot, Laurie, with Tom Cowan. *Power of the Witch: The Earth, the Moon and the Magical Path to Enlightenment.* New York: Dell Publishing, 1989.

Conway, D. J. *The Ancient & Shining Ones.* St. Paul, MN: Llewellyn Publications, 1993.

Cooper, Phillip. *Basic Magic: A Practical Guide.* York Beach, ME: Samuel Weiser, 1996.

Crowley, Aleister. *Magick in Theory and Practice.* New York: Dover Publications, 1976.

Cunningham, Scott. *Cunningham's Encyclopedia of Crystal, Gem & Metal Magic.* St. Paul, MN: Llewellyn Publications, 1992.

———. *Cunningham's Encyclopedia of Magical Herbs.* St. Paul, MN: Llewellyn Publications, 1985.

Davidson, Gustav. *A Dictionary of Angels, Including the Fallen Angels*. New York: The Free Press, 1967.

Denning, Melita, and Osborne Phillips. *Planetary Magick*. St. Paul, MN: Llewellyn Publications, 1989.

Dyer, Dr. Wayne W. *Real Magic: Creating Miracles in Everyday Life*. Audio cassette. New York: Harper Audio/HarperCollins Publishers, 1992.

Farrar, Janet and Stewart. *Spells and How They Work*. Custer, WA: Phoenix Publishing, 1990.

Goddard, David. *The Sacred Magic of the Angels*. York Beach, ME: Samuel Weiser, 1996.

Hay, Louise L. *Heal Your Body A-Z*. Carlsbad, CA: Hay House, 1988.

Harner, Michael. *The Way of the Shaman*. Third edition. New York: HarperCollins, 1990.

Hine, Phil. *Condensed Chaos*. Tempe, AZ: New Falcon, 1995.

Khalsa, Gurucharan Singh, Ph.D. *Happiness Is Your Birthright: The Complete Series*. Audio cassettes and guidebook. Wellesley, MA: Khalsa Consultants Inc., 1997.

Kraig, Donald Michael. *Modern Magick: Eleven Lessons in the High Magickal Arts*. St. Paul, MN: Llewellyn Publications, 1988.

The Kybalion: Hermetic Philosophy by Three Initiates. Chicago, IL: The Yogi Publication Society, 1912.

Medici, Marina. *Good Magic*. New York: Fireside Publishing, 1988.

Melody. *Love Is in the Earth*. Wheat Ridge, CO: Earth-Love Publishing, 1995.

Penczak, Christopher. *The Inner Temple of Witchcraft: Magick, Meditation and Psychic Development*. St. Paul, MN: Llewellyn Publications, 2002.

Valiente, Doreen. *Natural Magic*. Custer, WA: Phoenix Publishing, 1985.

Weed, Joseph J. *Wisdom of the Mystic Masters*. Prentice Hall Art, 1971.

Whitcomb, Bill. *The Magician's Companion*. St. Paul, MN: Llewellyn Publications, 1993.

Yin, Amorah Quan. *The Pleiadian Workbook: Awakening Your Divine Ka*. Santa Fe, NM: Bear & Company, 1996.

Index

akasha, 33, 36, 140, 142

alpha, 15–16

altered state, 15–17, 25, 34, 39, 44, 51, 56, 62–63, 106, 111, 122

ancestor, 39–40, 94, 119, 163, 192

angel, 38–40, 77, 79, 89, 96, 99, 106, 119, 161, 172–173, 192

Apophis, 42, 164

archetype, 31, 38, 54, 60

Ariadne, 41

astral, 32, 44, 49–50, 52, 69–72, 147–148, 156, 162, 165, 188, 192

Atropos, 41, 164

belly, 46–47, 51–53, 68, 75, 77, 79, 87, 90, 135, 140, 148–149, 165, 168–169

blade, 28, 34, 86, 96, 113–116, 124, 126, 162

body control, 132

body talking, 128, 151

Brahma, 42, 164, 182

breath, 16–18, 23–24, 32, 52–53, 92–93, 118, 134–138, 140, 142, 145, 157, 187

Breath of Fire, 134–136

brow, 48, 52–53, 136–137

Buffy the Vampire Slayer, 100

caduceus, 108–109

chakra, 46–49, 51–54, 60, 67–70, 72–75, 77–80, 82–85, 87, 89–90, 92–95, 97–99, 106, 108, 132, 136, 144, 148–150, 165, 168, 193

cleanse, 69–70, 79–80, 96–97, 116, 127–130

Clotho, 41, 164

coincidence, 65–66

color, 14, 25, 46, 58, 70, 78, 82–83, 94, 96–97, 102–103, 105–106, 108, 117, 123, 127, 144, 147–150, 168, 194

cone of power, 120

correspondence, 6, 9, 13, 30, 38, 45, 53, 60, 66–67, 84, 87, 100–103, 105, 111, 117, 126–127, 141, 161

creativity, 46, 54–55, 102, 126, 140, 165–168, 172, 182, 184, 186, 188–189, 195–197

crossroads, 36, 94, 178

crown, 16, 24, 47–48, 52–53, 74, 78, 84–85, 89, 91, 97, 140, 143, 165, 168, 193

cup, 34, 86, 100, 116, 125, 162

deity, 9–10, 38–39, 42, 44, 67–70, 72–80, 82–83, 85, 88–90, 92, 94, 96, 98–99,

102–103, 106, 108, 161, 163–164,
174–180, 182–183
demon, 38, 175
divine, 6, 17–22, 32–34, 36, 38–40, 48–51,
53, 55, 58, 60, 64, 86, 96–98, 102–103,
110, 115, 118–120, 122, 135, 140, 146,
157, 165, 169, 171, 174–175, 178, 180,
183–184, 187

earth (element), 17, 24, 31–35, 57, 66–68,
72, 78, 80–85, 87, 92, 99, 105–108,
117–118, 120, 139, 141–143, 152, 162,
168–171, 173, 175, 177, 182, 189,
195–196
elemental, 31–32, 34, 45, 49, 66, 69, 72,
74–75, 77, 84, 88, 105–107, 117–118,
120, 139–142, 148, 151–152, 170–171
elemental breathing, 138–139, 141, 144,
148
emotional, 25, 32, 46, 48–50, 52, 54, 70,
78, 86, 94, 126, 133, 149, 153, 162,
165–166, 172, 196–197
empowering, 125
energy, 1–2, 5–7, 9–10, 13–20, 22–36, 39,
43–45, 48, 50–57, 60, 62, 64, 66, 69–71,
76, 78–84, 89–94, 98–100, 103–108,
110–111, 113–120, 124–129, 132,
135–148, 152–154, 156–159, 161–162,
165–168, 170, 187–188, 192–197
etheric, 49–52, 71, 152, 165
ethics, 30, 64, 110

fate, 19, 21, 40, 90
fire (element), 17, 19, 31–35, 67, 72,
78–81, 85, 89, 91, 96, 99, 117–118, 120,
140–141, 152, 162, 168–170, 172,
175–176, 179, 181, 195, 197

God, 38, 42, 45, 55, 99, 102, 106–107, 119,
126, 175–183, 186
Goddess, 28, 40–41, 43–45, 53, 57, 81, 102,
108, 119, 126, 150, 175–182, 189, 192,
196

gold, 6, 57, 79, 82, 93, 126–127, 166, 169
Great Spirit, 118–119
grounding, 18, 82–84, 89, 124, 126, 134,
142, 154, 168–169, 189, 193, 195–196

healing, 1, 8, 34, 38, 54, 70, 78, 80–81, 88,
93–94, 97–98, 107–108, 110–111, 122,
126, 129, 131–154, 162–163, 165–166,
168–172, 175–176, 178, 181, 184–185,
188, 192–193, 195–197
heart, 17, 27, 35, 45, 47–48, 51–55, 61, 64,
72, 82, 85–87, 89, 94, 98–99, 108, 116,
119, 124, 140, 142–143, 148–149, 151,
159, 165, 168–169, 171, 192–193
higher self, 19, 48, 52–53, 55, 76, 111, 135,
146, 163, 165–166, 172

IAO, 42, 164
inner temple, 91, 101, 121–124, 153–154,
161, 174
intention, 6, 14, 18–22, 24–26, 28, 62,
66–75, 77–80, 82, 84–85, 87–90, 92–96,
98–99, 101–102, 105, 107–108, 111,
117, 119–120, 123, 125–129, 134,
143–145, 147–149, 153, 158, 197
iron, 85, 113, 126
Isis, 42, 70, 77–80, 82, 85, 89, 94, 96, 99,
164, 178–179, 181

Jupiter, 55, 58, 66, 69, 72, 78, 87, 89–90,
94–97, 99, 105–107, 126, 141, 166, 168,
173, 182–183

Karagoz, Mehmet, 10
kundalini yoga, 134–135

Lachesis, 41, 164
Law, 32
lead, 30, 45, 126–127, 158, 176
Liberty, 34
Life, 32
Light, 33
loa, 38

locations, 129
Love, 32
Lovecraft, H. P., 100
lower world, 36, 163

MacCool, Finn, 62
magick circle, 83, 115–118
magickal life, 66, 155–159
Mars, 54, 57–58, 70, 79, 85, 89, 96, 126, 166, 168, 173
meditation, 2, 15–16, 18, 35, 39, 44, 60, 81, 100–101, 103, 107, 114–115, 122, 129, 133, 137–138, 140–142, 148–150, 158, 172, 174
mental, 10, 25, 32, 34, 49–50, 52, 54, 57, 62, 70, 72, 78, 86, 92, 94, 118, 126, 131, 133, 149, 151, 162, 165, 193, 195
Mercury, 54, 57, 68–70, 72–75, 84, 87, 94, 105, 108–109, 126, 141–142, 166, 168, 172–173
Merlin, 34, 41, 70, 73–75, 88, 94, 97, 180
middle world, 36, 163
Moirae, 41, 90
moon, 6, 14, 38, 54, 57, 68, 70, 73, 77, 115, 119–120, 126, 143, 166, 168–169, 172, 175–176, 182, 187, 193, 196
mudra, 62–63, 141–142

negative breathing, 137–138
Neptune, 53, 55, 58, 84, 90, 92, 94, 98, 167–168, 172, 181
Norns, 41, 90

OM, 41–42
Osiris, 42, 77, 82, 85, 94, 96, 164, 178–179, 181

pagan, 1, 38, 174, 184
paradigm, 30–31, 36, 44, 60–61, 66, 74, 97, 104, 107, 111, 130, 139, 142, 158, 185
pathworking, 122
pentacle, 33–34, 80, 86, 114, 116, 124–125, 162, 171

pentagram, 34–36, 39, 44, 56, 71–72, 80, 97
physical, 8–10, 15–18, 25–26, 28–29, 31–33, 35, 46, 49–51, 53, 62, 67–68, 70, 80–81, 83, 86, 90, 107, 115, 121–122, 124–125, 131–133, 149–150, 152–153, 161–162, 165, 171, 173, 180, 184, 191–196
Pluto, 53, 55, 58, 60, 79, 94, 97, 167–169, 177
pore breathing, 143–145, 148
positive breathing, 137
prana, 24, 32, 142–143, 147–148, 152
Principle of Correspondence, 45
psychic, 48–50, 52, 54, 62, 66, 71, 78, 82, 89–91, 93, 101, 106, 115, 122, 125–126, 129, 146, 158, 165–166, 168–169, 172, 176, 180, 184, 187, 192–193, 196
psychic surgery, 152–154

quicksilver, 126

Rice, Anne, 100
ritual, 1, 5–7, 9–10, 13–17, 19–20, 23, 26–28, 31, 34, 36, 38, 42–43, 53–54, 60, 65, 78–80, 83–85, 88, 93–95, 97, 100, 102–106, 113–117, 119–122, 124–127, 129–131, 135, 156–157, 177
root, 46–47, 49, 51, 53, 67, 70, 78–80, 82, 84–85, 89, 93–94, 136, 165, 168–169

sacred space, 40, 85, 117, 119, 121–123, 129
Samantha, 63
Saturn, 55, 58, 67, 70, 78, 82–83, 85, 89, 93, 99, 105, 126, 141, 167, 169, 172–173, 176
shaman, 10, 36, 38, 55, 68
Shiva, 42, 69–70, 94, 98, 164, 182
silver, 6, 28, 57, 60, 77, 91, 97, 126–127, 162, 166, 169, 175
Sitalee Pranayam, 136
Skuld, 41, 164

solar plexus, 27, 46–47, 52–53, 73, 79, 85, 89, 135, 140, 165, 168–169

spell, 1–3, 5–9, 11, 13–28, 53–54, 61–104, 110–111, 113, 115–116, 119–122, 124–130, 139, 142, 144–146, 156–158, 161, 175, 186–190

spider, 40, 43, 80, 92–93, 189

spirit guide, 39–40, 93, 95, 102, 153, 192

spirit, 17, 31, 33–36, 38–40, 50, 60, 67–68, 74, 77, 83, 87–91, 93–96, 100, 103, 118–119, 124, 127–128, 140–142, 151, 158–159, 185–186, 188–189, 191–196

stone, 31, 67–68, 70, 72, 74, 76–77, 79, 83, 85–86, 88–89, 91, 94, 96, 99, 124–125, 127, 161–162, 194–197

Sufi, 138–139, 141, 144

sun, 6, 27, 29, 38, 43, 54, 57, 67, 72, 78, 116, 126, 140–141, 143, 166, 168–169, 172, 175–176, 178–179, 182, 186

Taliesin, 63, 74–75

technology, 14, 20, 26–27, 29, 73–74, 167, 177, 184

third eye, 47–48, 52, 73–74, 77–78, 84, 87, 90, 92, 94, 99, 136, 149, 165, 168, 193

thoughtforms, 25–26, 38, 100

throat, 47–48, 52–53, 68–69, 72–75, 87, 95, 99, 106, 132, 149, 165, 168

tin, 126

trance, 91, 133

Tree of Life, 59–60

trigger, 62–63, 69–72, 74–77, 82, 85, 87, 93, 96, 98, 101, 104–107, 114, 125, 128, 142, 150

triple goddess, 41, 176, 178

upper world, 36, 163, 192

Uranus, 53, 55, 58, 69, 72–73, 106, 167–168, 173, 183

Urd, 41, 164

Valiente, Doreen, 10

Venus, 53–54, 57, 82, 87, 95, 99, 108–109, 126, 141, 166, 168–169, 172, 175

Verdandi, 41, 164

Vishnu, 42, 164, 182

visualization, 2, 8, 23–24, 28, 79, 101–104, 107, 111, 124

ward, 130

water (element), 17, 28, 31–35, 73, 77, 82, 84, 89–92, 94, 97–98, 117–118, 120, 125, 139–141, 162, 168–172, 177, 181, 187, 193

web, 40, 43–45, 80, 92–93, 105

web of life, 40, 43–44

Weed, Joseph J., 137

Wicca, 6, 10, 23, 43, 64, 115, 119

will, 1, 5, 11, 19, 23–25, 29, 52, 64–65, 73, 91, 104, 106–107, 115, 117, 124, 143, 156, 159, 173, 197

world tree, 36–37, 40, 122–124, 154

Wyrd sisters, 41

To Write to the Author

If you wish to contact the author or would like more information about this book, please write to the author in care of Llewellyn Worldwide and we will forward your request. Both the author and publisher appreciate hearing from you and learning of your enjoyment of this book and how it has helped you. Llewellyn Worldwide cannot guarantee that every letter written to the author can be answered, but all will be forwarded. Please write to:

Christopher Penczak
℅ Llewellyn Worldwide
2143 Wooddale Drive, Dept. 0-7387-0859-3
Woodbury, Minnesota 55125-2989, U.S.A.
Please enclose a self-addressed stamped envelope for reply,
or $1.00 to cover costs. If outside U.S.A., enclose
international postal reply coupon.

Many of Llewellyn's authors have websites with additional information and resources. For more information, please visit our website at http://www.llewellyn.com.